INTERNATIONAL DEVELOPMENT IN FOCUS

Which Way to Livable and Productive Cities?
A Road Map for Sub-Saharan Africa

Kirsten Hommann and Somik V. Lall

⊕ **WORLD BANK GROUP**

Contents

Acknowledgments

This policy note was prepared by Kirsten Hommann and Somik V. Lall, under the overall guidance of Meskerem Brhane and Bernice van Bronkhorst. It draws on the volume of research papers, urbanization reviews, and the following background notes prepared specifically to inform this overview: poverty and services (Shohei Nakamura, Bhavya Paliwal, and Nobuo Yoshida); fertility and migration (Olivia d'Aoust and Hannah Kim); urbanization and the economy (Angus Kathage); livability and the environment (Hannah Kim and Bontje Zangerling), finance and institutions (William Dillinger and Roland White), and urban planning and land (Peter Ellis, Chyi-Yun Huang, Qingyun Shen, and Bontje Zangerling). Judy Baker, Kathleen Beegle, Luc Christiaensen, Andrew Dabalen, Ruth Hill, Dino Merotto, and Albert Zeufack provided helpful guidance, information, and comments; and Alex Chunet provided invaluable inputs. Sonia Wheeler supported the team administratively throughout the process.

Numerical Highlights

- Sub-Saharan Africa's urban population doubled since the mid-1990s, reaching almost 400 million in 2016. The share of urban population rose from 31 percent in 2000, to 40 percent in 2017.
- Nearly three-fourths (72 percent) of the region's urban population resides in urban areas outside the largest city of each country.
- The rapid increase in Sub-Saharan Africa's urban population in recent years is largely attributed to natural growth, and rural-to-urban migration is estimated to contribute less than 40 percent.
- Although the urban poverty head-count ratio (22 percent) is less than half the rural poverty head-count ratio (47 percent), the number of urban poor has been increasing, because of urban population growth.
- Already 60 percent of Sub-Saharan Africa's urban population lives in areas classified as slums by the United Nations Human Settlements Programme, a far larger share than the average of 34 percent in other developing countries.
- Just under 25 percent of urban households in Sub-Saharan Africa has access to piped water, and about 35 percent use a flush toilet.
- African households rely on getting to their jobs on foot: more than 50 percent of trips are done by walking in Bamako, Conakry, Dakar, Douala, and Niamey.
- Today, large cities of more than 1 million people account for 34 percent of Sub-Saharan Africa's urban population; secondary cities of 250,000 to 1 million for about 15 percent; but, most striking, smaller cities and towns with fewer than 250,000 people for about 50 percent. Small towns with fewer than 50,000 people account for 29 percent.
- More than 25 percent of the urban population is employed in agriculture, compared with 10 percent outside Sub-Saharan Africa.
- More than 4 million urban residents were estimated to live in Sub-Saharan Africa's low-elevation coastal zones in 2000. That number is expected to reach 26 million by 2030, and 110 million by 2060.

Policy Highlights

- Urban livability and prosperity cannot be pursued effectively without distinguishing larger cities from smaller towns.
- To become economically dense, efficient, and productive, cities require functioning land markets with formal ownership records and transfer procedures. Rural areas and their peri-urban small towns equally require land markets to function to enable mechanisms for consolidating land parcels in response to demand and to become more competitive.
- Planning is needed across the urban space—in the smaller towns to avoid the damage from encroachment and the urban sprawl already inflicted on larger cities, and in the larger cities to use land better by making cities denser and better connected, better serviced, and better functioning.
- Infrastructure investment decisions need to be informed by appropriate investment planning to better identify, appraise, and monitor investment projects. Instituting better systems for public investment management is essential across urban institutions, and its principles need to be applied to intergovernmental transfers as well as direct investments.
- Policy actions for small towns are not that different from large cities, with most of the differences a matter of degree and delivery.
  - The lack of institutional capacity in the smaller towns may require a slower transition of responsibilities for planning and investment management, as well as enhanced technical assistance so that institutions can perform their tasks.
  - Infrastructure requirements in smaller towns are far lower in terms of capital investments than in larger cities, because service solutions can be more decentralized at the household level rather than requiring collective systems that are more expensive.
  - Small-town investments are likely to be less bankable, and thus need to be supported through public funds or external aid, whereas larger cities may have bankable projects that can crowd in more private finance.

Abbreviations

BRT	bus rapid transit
CSRM	census survival ratio method
GDP	gross domestic product
GIS	geographical information system
LECZ	low-elevation coastal zone
NP	nonpoor
PIM	public investment management
PPP	purchasing power parity; public-private partnership
TFR	total fertility rate
URPAS	urban-rural population by age and sex

Overview

Urban population growth is in full stride in Sub-Saharan Africa, but it has done less to reduce poverty than might be expected. To be sure, a poor person in any urban settlement generally has greater access to all sorts of services than a non-poor person in a rural area. Unlike in other regions, however, urbanization in Sub-Saharan Africa has not generated the economic growth to bring poverty numbers down faster.

Despite its high urban growth, Sub-Saharan Africa is experiencing low urbanization. Sub-Saharan Africa's urban population doubled since the mid-1990s, reaching almost 400 million in 2016. The share of urban population rose from 31 percent in 2000 to 40 percent in 2017, but much of that population growth was a natural effect of fertility, not an economic effect involving migration. The share of urban population residing in the largest cities remained almost steady over that period. Much larger increases can be recorded in urban areas outside the largest cities; these increases are due to a combination of natural growth, rural-to-urban migration, and reclassifying rural areas as urban.

Poverty is urbanizing, with the share of urban poor in the total number of poor on the rise. Although the urban poverty head-count ratio (22 percent) is less than half the rural poverty head-count ratio (47 percent), the number of urban poor has been increasing because of urban population growth. In tandem, the share of urban poor in the total number of poor has been rising slightly, contributing to a massive increase in income inequality within cities and towns.

When cities function well, they are the engines of economic growth and prosperity. No country has reached middle income without urbanizing. Economic development in the West and more recently in the East Asian growth miracles was achieved through structural transformations that started with the move of agricultural labor to higher-productivity jobs in urban manufacturing and services. The tremendous power of cities to drive productivity growth stems from agglomeration—the clustering of businesses and individuals in an environment that promotes scale and specialization. Population densities bring workers closer to jobs, increasing workers' opportunities and fueling their productivity. Cities and towns bring people physically closer, facilitating the exchange of ideas and bringing about innovations. In Sub-Saharan Africa, cities generate about one-third of national gross domestic product (GDP), but they are not creating enough jobs for the large youth population that is waiting to work.

The density of well-planned cities enables efficient public service provision. Well-planned cities and towns are compact. They have an organized road layout along which public infrastructure can be sunk, and they use land efficiently, with more intensity in the inner core. Such spatial form reduces the cost per person to lay the infrastructure for roads, utilities, and mass transit, thus enabling better service provision and connectivity. High densities make it cheaper to provide services efficiently and equitably. For these reasons, two important benefits of urban life—productivity and livability—are associated with proximity within the city. However, urban development in many African cities is fragmented, making them less livable and productive.

In Sub-Saharan Africa, urban population growth has far outpaced capital investment, leading to shortages of all types of infrastructure and housing. Already 60 percent of Sub-Saharan Africa's urban population lives in areas classified as slums by the United Nations Human Settlements Programme (Lall, Henderson, and Venables 2017), a far larger share than the average of 34 percent in other developing countries (UN DESA 2015). At current rates of population growth, this number will increase unless sizable investments are made in infrastructure and affordable housing. Households within the lowest consumption quintile, spending 60 percent of their incomes on food (Lozano-Gracia and Young 2014), are unable to afford formal housing and have no choice but either to live in slums within or close to the town or city center or to live at the periphery of cities and towns, where they cannot connect to jobs.

How a city is spatially configured and the infrastructure it offers are key determinants of whether it can generate and promote competitive industries. The spatial development of African cities is constrained because they are more crowded, disconnected, and costly (Lall, Henderson, and Venables 2017). They are not economically dense, and investments in infrastructure, industrial, and commercial structures have not kept pace with the concentration of people. Instead, cities have developed as collections of small and fragmented neighborhoods, limiting workers' job opportunities and preventing firms from reaping the benefits of scale and agglomeration (Lall, Henderson, and Venables 2017). And they are expensive—55 percent of Sub-Saharan households face higher costs relative to households in other countries with a comparable per capita GDP. This high cost of living raises nominal wages and transaction costs, making African industries less competitive both regionally and internationally.

For African cities to grow economically as they have grown in size, they must create productive environments to attract investments, increase economic efficiency, and create livable environments that prevent urban costs from rising with increased population densification. For Sub-Saharan Africa's largest cities to take advantage of agglomeration forces, policy makers will need to resolve basic structural problems and improve conditions for both people and businesses.

Urban growth—if unchecked and unmanaged—causes ecosystem loss that increases a city's vulnerabilities and negative externalities. *Vulnerabilities* rise as environmental degradation reduces a city's capacity to absorb shocks of a "wet event" or prolonged "dry events" (Henderson, Storeygard, and Deichmann 2017). Exposure to risk, especially by the urban poor, has increased with rapid population growth and encroachment on wetlands, floodplains, riverbanks, steep slopes, and other hazard-prone areas. Many risks are exacerbated by climate change. Whereas some damages can be repaired in the future with additional infrastructure—assuming adequate finance and capacity—others are irreversible and will reduce the prospects of future generations.

Negative externalities emerge as low infrastructure investment and insufficient service delivery lead to pollution, flooding, and overconsumption of resources. When people move to cities, their direct dependence on natural resources usually declines with increased income opportunities; however, in Sub-Saharan Africa, most urban poor live in informal settlements and depend more on natural systems to meet their basic needs (especially in peri-urban areas). Many still rely on agriculture and on firewood, biofuels, and water, the excessive use of which harms the surrounding environment from which they are sourced, and leads to localized problems of environmental degradation and pollution.

The challenges of urban livability and prosperity—with the realities of demographic transition and the urgent need for an environmentally sustainable economic transformation—cannot be clarified without distinguishing larger cities from smaller towns: because they are different, they offer very different opportunities and challenges, and they require different policy solutions and investments. Today, nearly three-fourths (72 percent) of the region's urban population resides in urban areas outside the largest city of each country. The challenge is to enable all cities and towns within the urban hierarchy to deliver functions and services that are commensurate with their size and opportunities.

What are the central obstacles that prevent Sub-Saharan Africa's cities and towns from becoming sustainable engines of economic growth and prosperity? Among the most critical factors that limit the growth and livability of urban areas are land markets, investments in public infrastructure and assets, and the institutions to enable both.

- Land registration and transaction remain a challenge across most African countries, with the result that land is not allocated efficiently and to its best use. Also, urban land is often encroached upon, limiting infrastructure investments and reducing service availability, connectivity, and recreational spaces.
- City and town governments have limited administrative remit over many of the issues pertaining to their locality, and this limitation is further aggravated by inadequate institutional capabilities where they have such remit. One such important function of city governments is urban planning, which is the glue that binds capital investments to the function of land.
- The lack of even basic infrastructure in most African cities (like piped water, sewage, or environmentally sound landfills) requires capital investments at scale and innovative thinking about how to crowd in finance beyond donor aid.

To unleash the potential of African cities and towns for delivering services and employment in a livable and environmentally friendly environment, a sequenced approach is needed to reform institutions and policies and to target infrastructure investments. Three foundations need fixing to guide cities and towns throughout Sub-Saharan Africa on their way to productivity and livability:

1. *Empowering land markets*—to drive urban economic growth and promote economic density. To realize agglomeration effects from efficient urban land use, land rights must be formal, readily transferrable, and subject to consolidation as far as is consistent with optimal zoning.
2. *Strengthening urban planning and regulatory functions*—to make both market-driven growth and coordinated investments possible.

3. *Financing for public assets and infrastructure investments*—to promote urban agglomeration effects from efficiency and connectivity, at the same time making urban settlements environmentally sustainable. Early targeted investments could enable efficient matching of workers with jobs, link firms with markets, and connect commuters to their workplaces and schools, while guarding against and mitigating vulnerabilities and negative externalities from urban growth.

MAIN MESSAGES

In the long term, urbanization should reduce poverty and improve lives in three ways:

1. *By enhancing productivity:* Enhancing workers' productivity and thus wages through economic transformation happens both through the release of agricultural workers to the urban sector (thus enhancing agricultural productivity) and through specialization and other agglomeration benefits.
2. *By improving amenities:* Economies of scale in service provision improve livability and amenities throughout the urban space.
3. *By reducing negative externalities:* Providing better living conditions and options for getting out of poverty eases pressure on natural capital resources.

In the short to medium term, however, Sub-Saharan Africa's cities and towns face hurdles that—unless overcome—will block their paths to urbanization's long-term benefits. This report sets forth three pillars that should guide governments in Sub-Saharan Africa as they chart their diverse paths toward livable cities.

1. *Empowering land markets*—to drive urban economic growth and promote economic density.
2. *Strengthening urban planning and regulation*—to make market-driven growth and coordinated investments possible.
3. *Financing public assets and infrastructure investments*—to promote urban agglomeration effects from efficiency and connectivity while guarding against and mitigating vulnerabilities and negative externalities.

REFERENCES

Henderson, V., A. Storeygard, and U. Deichmann. 2017. "Has Climate Change Driven Urbanization in Africa?" *Journal of Development Economics* 124 (C): 60–82.

Lall, S., J. Henderson, and A. Venables. 2017. *Africa's Cities: Opening Doors to the World.* Washington, DC: World Bank.

Lozano-Gracia, N., and C. Young. 2014. "Housing Consumption and Urbanization." Policy Research Working Paper 7112, World Bank, Washington, DC.

UN DESA (United Nations Department of Economic and Social Affairs). 2015. "Indicator 7.10: Proportion of Urban Population Living in Slums." Millenium Development Goals Indicators (database). New York: UNDESA. http://mdgs.un.org/unsd/mdg/seriesdetail .aspx?srid=710.

1 Cities and Towns Are Growing, yet the Potential Benefits of Urbanization Remain Distant

Sub-Saharan Africa is experiencing high urban population growth but low urbanization. By 2040, half the Sub-Saharan population is expected to live in an urban area. Urban population growth, triggered by both natural increase and migration, would thus translate into adding 40,000 new urban citizens every day until 2040 (World Bank 2013).

SUB-SAHARAN AFRICA IS URBANIZING, WHILE POOR AND LOW WEALTH MEAN WEAK INSTITUTIONS AND LAGGING INVESTMENTS

Sub-Saharan Africa is far poorer than other regions were when they reached similar urbanization levels. To the extent that Sub-Saharan Africa is urbanizing, it is doing so at a much lower income level than other regions historically (figure 1.1). Today 40 percent of Sub-Saharan Africa's population lives in an urban area, and average per capita gross domestic product (GDP) amounts to just above US$1,000. When the Middle East and North Africa region reached the 40 percent mark in 1968, its per capita GDP was nearly twice that level at US$1,800. When East Asia reached 40 percent urbanization in 1994, its GDP per capita was US$3,600.

Low income means that Sub-Saharan Africa's urbanization is not accompanied by critical infrastructure investments, posing some of its biggest challenges. To take just housing and transport as examples, the challenges include an increasing number of people living in informal and hazardous settlements and an ever-expanding urban footprint that increases the cost of commuting, lowers the economies of scale of service provision, and raises the costs of doing business, making cities uncompetitive.

Fewer resources also mean underinvestment in human capital and related physical capital. Cities need schools, health clinics, and other infrastructure services besides transport and housing. Without such investments, agglomeration

FIGURE 1.1

FIGURE 1.1

Sub-Saharan Africa is urbanizing at lower per capita GDPs than other regions

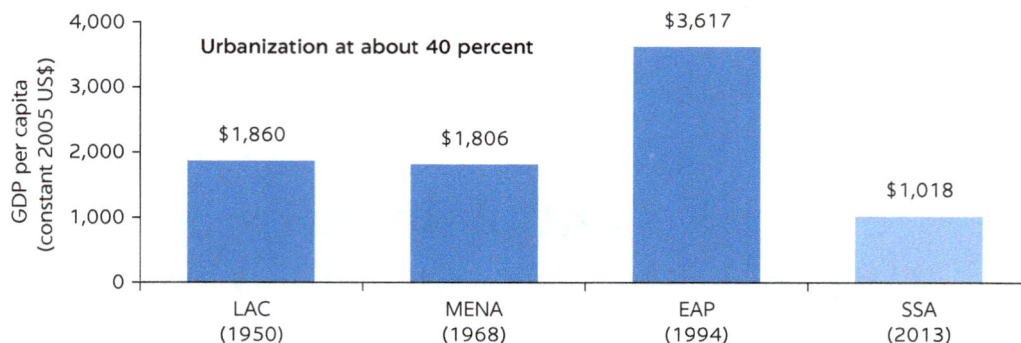

Source: Lall, Henderson, and Venables 2017.
Note: EAP = East Asia and Pacific; LAC = Latin America and the Caribbean; MENA = Middle East and North Africa; SSA = Sub-Saharan Africa.

benefits cannot be reaped because the workforce does not receive needed education to match skills with employment requirements. Institutional improvements are stalled, and the overall population remains poorly served.

URBANIZATION HAS NOT BEEN ASSOCIATED WITH THE ECONOMIC GROWTH EXPERIENCED ELSEWHERE

Urbanization has traditionally been strongly correlated with the expansion of manufacturing, engendering an increase of per capita income growth. For most countries, manufacturing as a share of GDP rises with urban shares until about 60 percent of the population lives in cities and manufacturing accounts for about 15 percent of GDP (Lall, Henderson, and Venables 2017). Most Sub-Saharan countries have not seen large reallocation of economic activity from the agricultural sector toward the more productive industrial and service sectors, and this has resulted in urbanization without growth (figure 1.2).

URBANIZATION HAS DONE LITTLE TO REDUCE POVERTY IN MOST SUB-SAHARAN COUNTRIES, BECAUSE MOST URBAN POPULATION GROWTH IN SUB-SAHARAN AFRICA IS A NATURAL EFFECT OF FERTILITY, NOT AN ECONOMIC PULL INDUCING MIGRATION

The relation of urbanization to poverty in Sub-Saharan Africa presents a paradox. Poverty is substantially lower in urban than in rural areas, and, although poverty is falling in the region overall, it is declining fastest in large cities (box 1.1). Even so, research suggests that urbanization—or the rising urban share of the population—has played only a small role in overall poverty reduction. How can that be?

One explanation is that urban population growth in Sub-Saharan Africa is driven not by migration to cities but by fertility (a factor that also persists in rural Sub-Saharan Africa). Most urban growth in Sub-Saharan Africa thus comes from a natural dynamic—not an economic one. Although poverty has

FIGURE 1.2

Urbanization has been associated with uniform growth in East Asia, but the story is a mixed bag for Sub-Saharan Africa

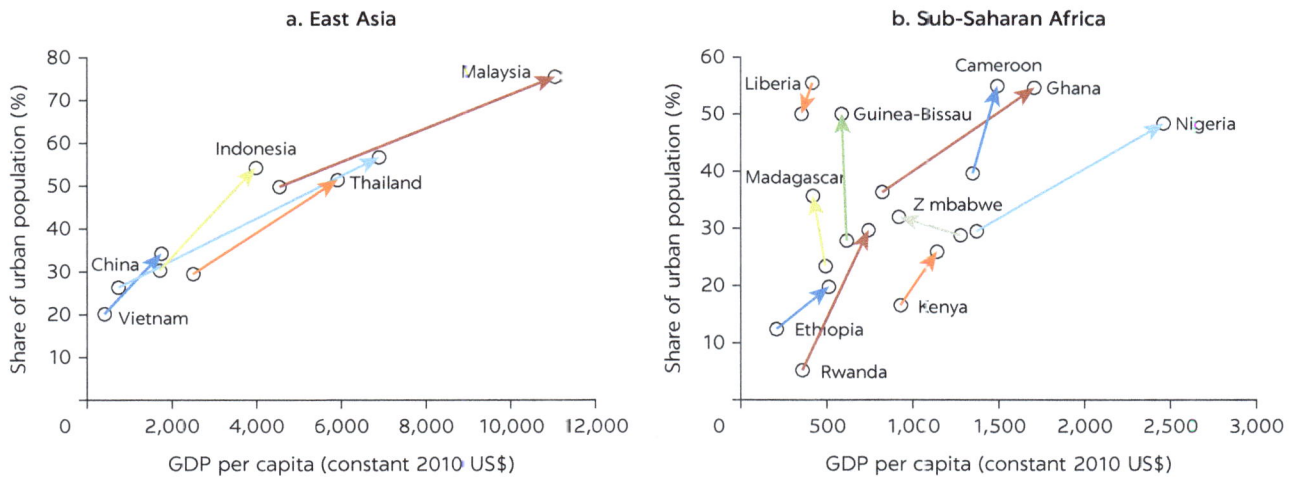

a. East Asia

b. Sub-Saharan Africa

Source: Calculations based on World Development Indicators.
Note: Data correspond to changes between 1990 and 2016.

BOX 1.1

Although declining across Africa, poverty has declined faster in large cities than in rural or other urban areas

Since 2000, poverty head-count ratios have declined across Sub-Saharan Africa as a whole. Nevertheless, they have been significantly and consistently lower in the largest cities than in other urban or rural areas—or across national populations (figure B1.1.1). The absolute numbers of poor are declining in capital cities—while rising in other urban areas.

Why is poverty declining faster in large cities? Moving from a rural area to an urban one is associated with a differential of improved access to water, sanitation, and electricity of about 45, 35, and 50 percent, respectively; and, despite rapid urban population growth, the share of the poor in total urban population (the urban poverty head-count ratio) has been declining faster in urban than in rural areas of Sub-Saharan Africa. In fact, this share has been decreasing even faster in the largest cities than in smaller towns—though not in pure numbers.

Urbanization, however, accounts for only a small fraction of poverty reduction in Sub-Saharan

Africa. In recent years, only a few Sub-Saharan countries have harnessed urbanization for poverty reduction (figure B1.1.2). Analyzing the contribution of urbanization to poverty reduction, overall poverty reduction can be decomposed into an intra-sectoral effect, a population-shift effect, and residuals. The *intrasectoral effect* estimates what would have happened with the overall poverty head-count ratio if the urban/rural population shares remained constant and only the level of poverty within urban/rural areas changed (no rural–urban population shift). The *population-shift effect* estimates what would have happened with the overall poverty head-count if the respective rural and urban poverty rates had remained constant and the only change that occured was in the urban/rural population share (that is, no change in poverty within urban/rural).[a]

For example, although Tanzania reduced its poverty head-count ratio by 4.4 percentage points every

continued

Box 1.1, *continued*

FIGURE B1.1.1

Poverty head-count ratios and the number of poor, 2000–14

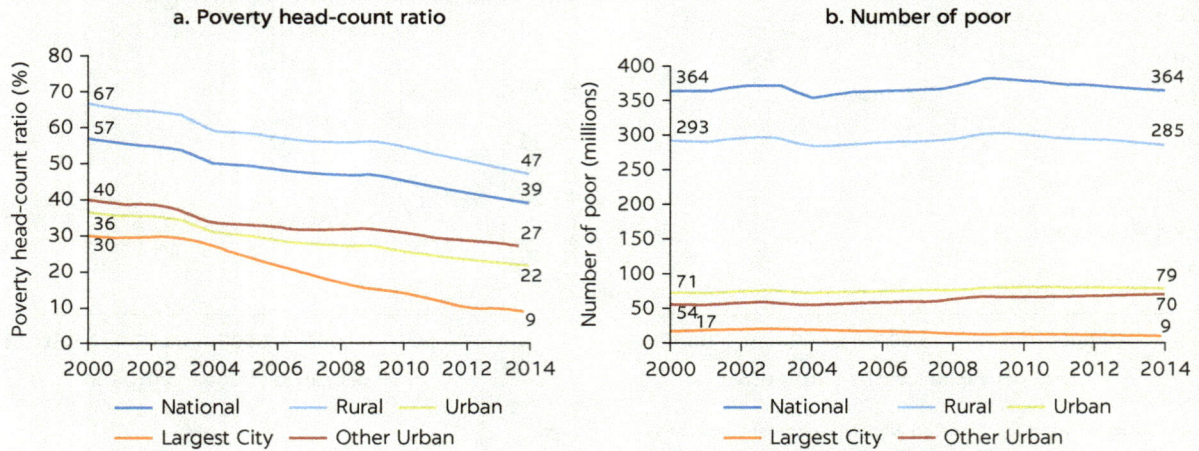

a. Poverty head-count ratio

b. Number of poor

Source: Nakamura, Paliwal, and Yoshida 2018.
Note: Trends are based on population-weighted country-level poverty head-count ratios. Poverty is measured by the international poverty line (US$1.90 a day, 2011 purchasing power parity [PPP]) for the analytical purpose, and this measure is not exactly the same as the official World Bank estimate. Lack of spatial price adjustments when applying the $PPP international poverty line may result in overestimating rural poverty and underestimating urban poverty.

FIGURE B1.1.2

Only a few countries managed to translate urbanization to poverty reduction

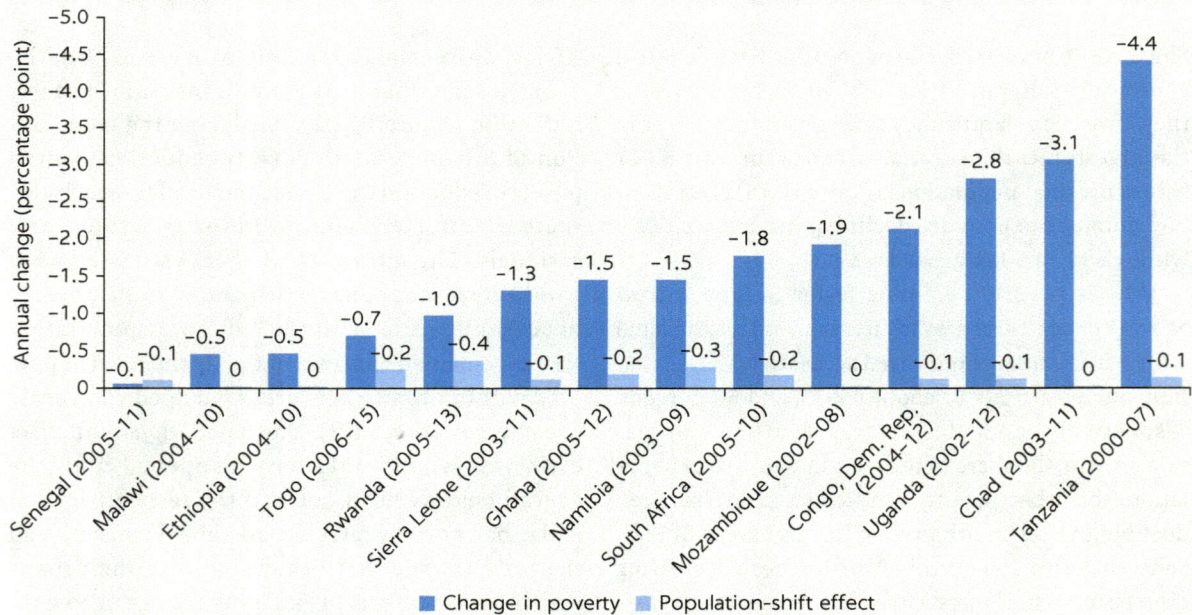

Sources: Nakamura, Paliwal, and Yoshida 2018; Ravallion and Huppi 1991.
Note: Change in poverty head-count ratio between two survey periods is decomposed into (1) rural and urban population-shift effects, (2) within urban/rural poverty reduction, and (3) residuals. Figure shows annualized percent change in poverty head-count ratio and annualized population-shift effect. Figure shows only countries that have two comparable surveys and reduced poverty between circa 2002 and circa 2012.

continued

Box 1.1, *continued*

year between 2000 and 2007, a rural-to-urban population shift reduced the poverty head-count ratio by
only 0.1 percentage point annually (3 percent contribution to overall poverty reduction). In contrast,

among the countries analyzed, Ghana, Namibia,
Rwanda, and Togo have been relatively successful in
translating urbanization to poverty reduction (a more
than 10 percent contribution).

a. This population-shift effect does not consider either selection bias in migration—that is, only rural residents who would have been
successful in rural areas anyway migrated from rural to urban areas—or spillover effects—the economies in urbanizing areas benefitted
nearby rural villages. Still, this accounting exercise offers useful insight in understanding the link between urbanization and poverty
reduction.

declined in cities, its decline has little to do with the economic potential inherent
in efficient urban agglomerations—a potential that generally is not being realized.

Urban population growth is not driven by traditional "push and pull"
migration. Although rural-to-urban migration has occurred for decades, the
rapid increase in Africa's urban population in recent years is largely attributed to
natural growth; rural-to-urban migration is estimated to contribute less than
40 percent (Jedwab, Christiansen, and Gindelsy 2017). Standard models explain
rural-to-urban migration by a combination of a *rural push*—conflict, drought,
unemployment, and poverty—and an *urban pull*, when better prospects of
income and living conditions make people move to urban centers. Increasingly,
however, research has pointed to the stalling demographic transition in explain-
ing urban growth rates.

Compared with other developing regions, Sub-Saharan Africa's urban fertility rates are declining slowly, though there is a fair bit of variation by country.
Medical progress has significantly reduced mortality rates across Sub-Saharan
countries, especially in cities, but fertility remains a choice dependent on wom-
en's education, employment opportunities, and wider access to the media and
information. Fertility is thus lower in larger cities than in smaller towns and
rural areas. The decline in fertility seems to have stalled, however, in the largest
cities—such as Accra, Bamako, Banjul, Brazzaville, Cotonou, Dar es Salaam,
Harare, Kampala, Kinshasa, Lagos, Libreville, Lomé, Nairobi, Niamey, and
Yaoundé/Douala—whereas fertility in all other cities is continuing its decline,
albeit slowly in several (see figure 1.3 for a subset of country analyses).

Where fertility rates are not declining fast enough or are stalling, natural
growth has become an increasing factor in driving urban population growth.
Although the picture varies by subregion, the overall trends for Sub-Saharan
Africa, from the least urbanized East to the more urbanized South, show a
decline in the contribution of net in-migration to urban growth in favor of the
natural growth component (figure 1.4).[1] In the least urbanized East African subregion (25 percent average urbanization in 2015), migration contributes the most
to urban population growth and about twice as much as natural growth. In contrast, in the more urbanized Southern African subregion (60 percent urbanized
in 2015), the contribution of net migration to urban population growth became
negative around 1995, meaning that more urban residents were leaving cities for
rural areas than rural residents leaving for cities.

FIGURE 1.3

Urban fertility declines are stalling in some countries, continuing slowly in others

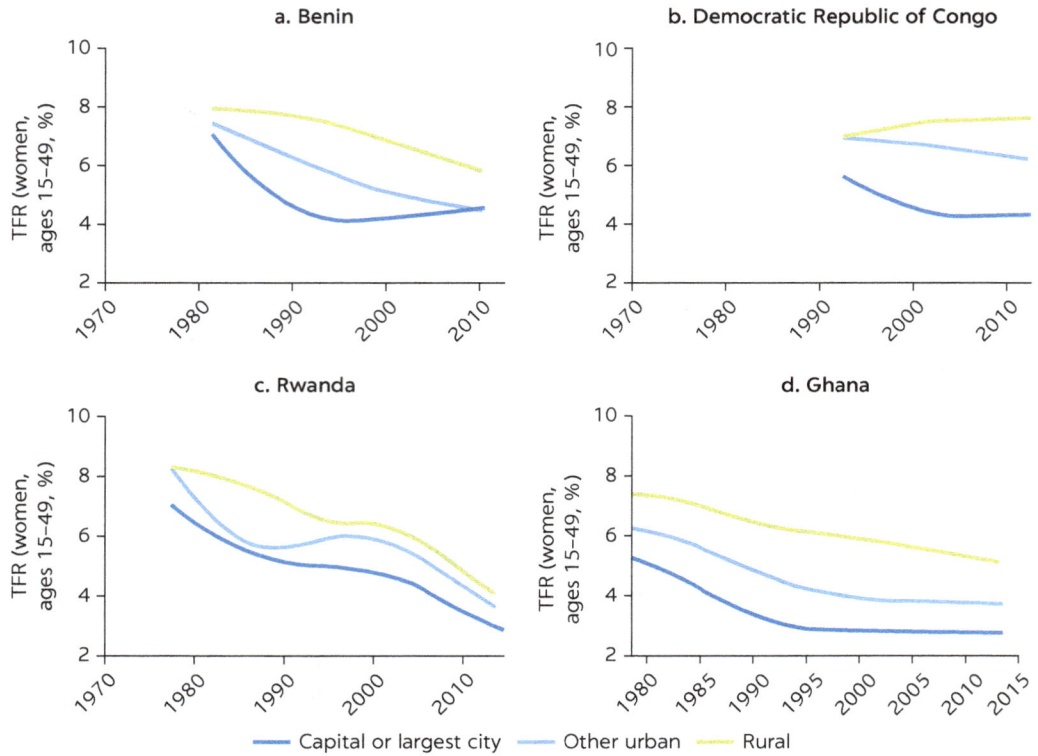

a. Benin

b. Democratic Republic of Congo

c. Rwanda

d. Ghana

— Capital or largest city — Other urban — Rural

Source: Bocquier and Schoumaker, forthcoming.
Note: Total fertility rates (TFRs) are reported as trends constructed by pooling birth histories from successive surveys and smoothed with restricted cubic splines.

Some African cities are contending with a large influx of refugees and internally displaced persons, which has contributed to temporal population increases. Managing the shock caused by an inflow of forcibly displaced persons creates both risks and opportunities for host communities. As large numbers are forced to flee from their homes because of conflict and violence, most have been hosted by African countries. In some exceptional cases, this influx creates new dynamics for the entire host country, and national development strategies must be adjusted accordingly. It therefore becomes important for host communities to manage these new circumstances so that they can continue to reduce poverty while providing an accepting environment for the forcibly displaced.

Although urban residents are, on average, more well-off than those in rural areas, inequality in service access is on the rise. In large cities declining poverty comes at the cost of increased inequality. Access to better infrastructure services like piped water, flush toilets, and electricity appears more unequal in urban than in rural settlements (figure 1.5), where such services are often not available to start with. In contrast, the gap in service access to improved water between the poor and nonpoor (P and NP in the figure) is less pronounced in towns or cities, but it has been increasing in rural areas. As one would expect, the opposite is the case for improved sanitation, for which access is less equal in urban settings—mostly because of lack of space—than in rural areas. However, and

FIGURE 1.4

Natural increase contributes more than in-migration to urban population growth

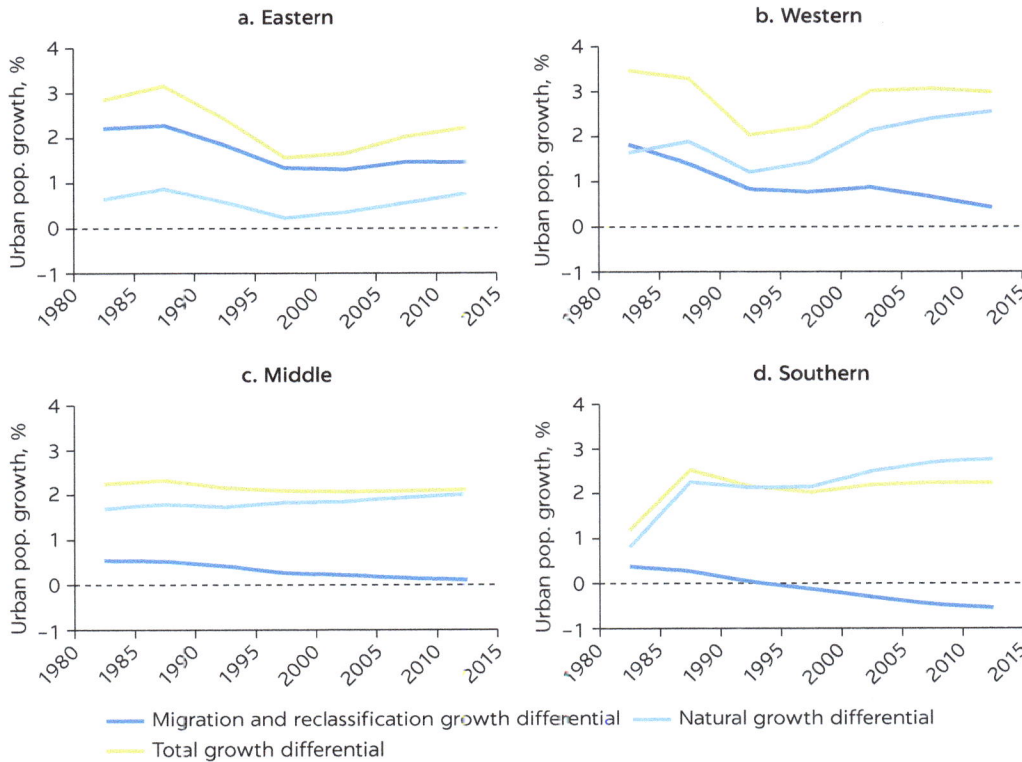

a. Eastern

b. Western

c. Middle

d. Southern

—— Migration and reclassification growth differential —— Natural growth differential
—— Total growth differential

Source: Bocquier and Schoumaker, forthcoming.
Note: The panels above show the total urban population growth rate across different regions in Sub-Saharan Africa (total growth differential). The total urban growth rate is further decomposed into the portion attributable to natural growth (natural growth differential) and the one driven by migration and reclassification (migration and reclassification growth differential), by applying the census survival ratio method (CSRM) to urban-rural population by age and sex (URPAS) provided by the United Nations for five-year intervals over the period 1980–2015 for 45 Sub-Saharan countries.

irrespective of inequality within towns or cities, being poor in an urban area—town or city—is associated with access to all types of services that is far better than that of the nonpoor in rural areas.

Evidence is inconclusive on the gains in real net income when people move from rural to urban areas and when taking into consideration the costs of living. Henderson and Kriticos (2017) compare real income differences across settlements in the urban hierarchy in three countries, and their results are diverse: in Uganda, moving from a rural area to a small town has been estimated to maximize income; by contrast, moving to Kampala yields a lower net income premium because higher housing rents erode the income differential. In Nigeria and Tanzania, the highest income gains are reaped when people move to the largest cities; however, these gains do not take into account housing rents (figure 1.6) (Henderson and Kriticos 2017). Further, and without controlling for any living cost differentials, analyzing earnings across capital city, other urban, and rural areas in Côte d'Ivoire points to nominal wage differences being more moderate among workers with lower education levels. Among the better educated, earnings in urban areas are nearly three times rural agriculture wages (see table 2.1 in Christiaensen and Premand 2017).

FIGURE 1.5

The urban poor are better served than the rural nonpoor

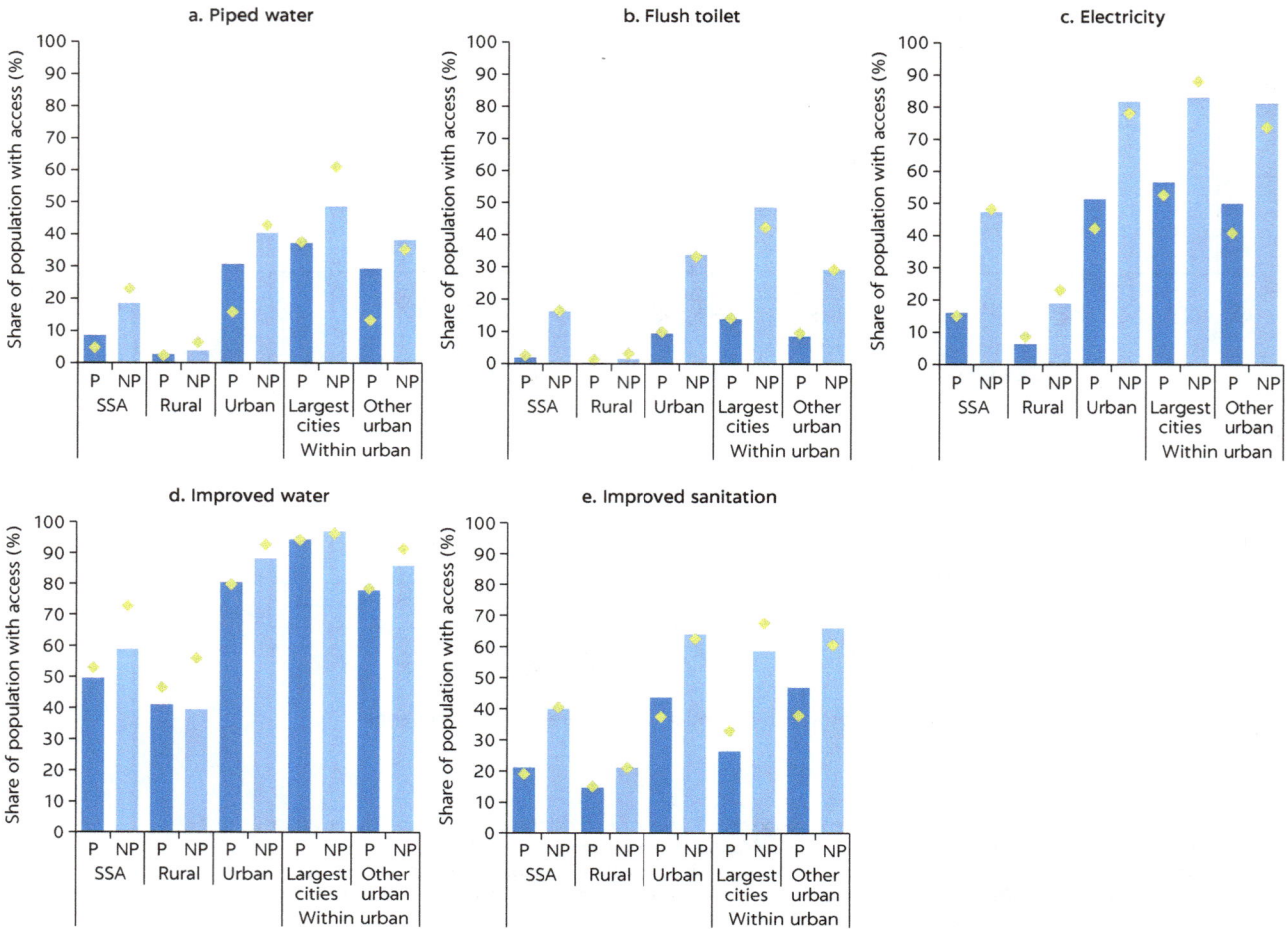

a. Piped water

Share of population with access (%)

P NP | P NP | P NP | P NP | P NP
SSA | Rural | Urban | Largest cities | Other urban
Within urban

b. Flush toilet

Share of population with access (%)

P NP | P NP | P NP | P NP | P NP
SSA | Rural | Urban | Largest cities | Other urban
Within urban

c. Electricity

Share of population with access (%)

P NP | P NP | P NP | P NP | P NP
SSA | Rural | Urban | Largest cities | Other urban
Within urban

d. Improved water

Share of population with access (%)

P NP | P NP | P NP | P NP | P NP
SSA | Rural | Urban | Largest cities | Other urban
Within urban

e. Improved sanitation

Share of population with access (%)

P NP | P NP | P NP | P NP | P NP
SSA | Rural | Urban | Largest cities | Other urban
Within urban

Source: Nakamura, Paliwal, and Yoshida 2018.
Note: Diamond markers indicate the population share with access in circa 2012; bars indicate the population share with access in circa 2005. Poverty is measured by the international poverty line (US$1.90 per capita a day, 2011 purchasing power parity). NP = nonpoor; P = poor; SSA = Sub-Saharan Africa.

FIGURE 1.6

Net wage premiums vary across the urban hierarchy

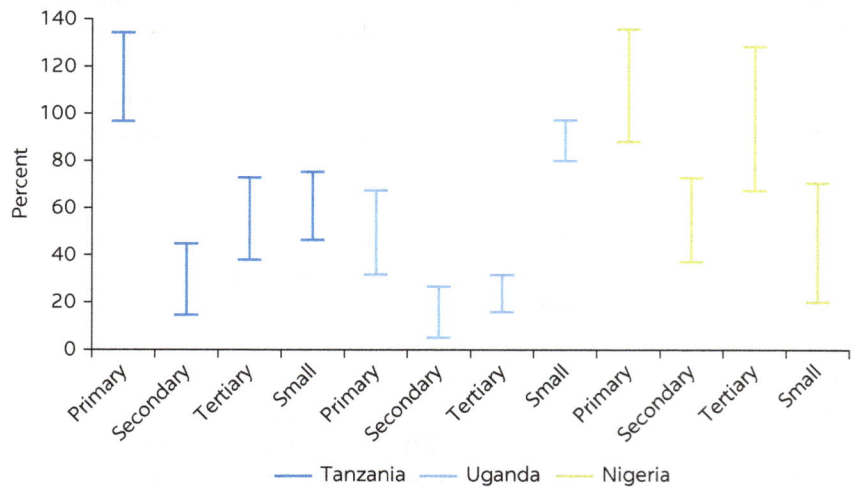

Percent

Primary | Secondary | Tertiary | Small | Primary | Secondary | Tertiary | Small | Primary | Secondary | Tertiary | Small

—— Tanzania —— Uganda —— Nigeria

Source: Henderson and Kriticos 2017.

FIGURE 1.7

Spending on food is high for all urban households and across all expenditure quintiles

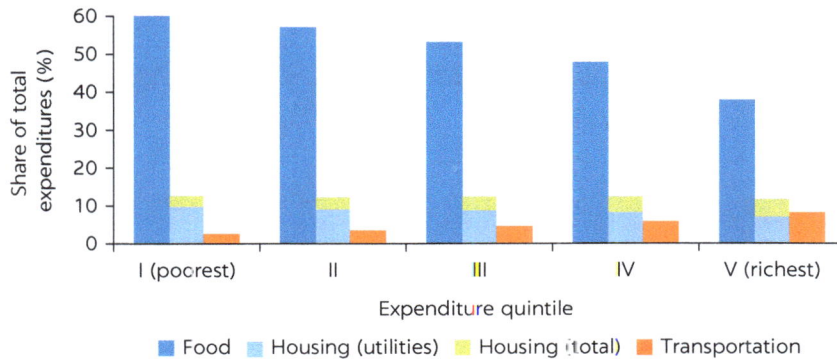

Source: Lozano-Gracia and Young 2014.

Generally, the higher expense of living in urban areas limits the net real income difference between rural and urban. Although not as expensive as living in large cities, urban living in general involves higher costs for housing, land, services, local taxes, and food (if not self-produced) than does living in rural areas. Households in Sub-Saharan Africa's large cities spent, on average, about 50 percent of their income on food, more than 10 percent on housing, and 5 percent on transportation (figure 1.7). The share of expenditure for the poorest of urban households on food reaches an exorbitant 60 percent, leaving little room for much else. Housing shares, by contrast, are surprisingly equal across quintiles; however, patterns vary across countries—poorer households allocate a higher share of budget for housing than richer households in Malawi and Uganda, whereas richer households allocate more in Angola and Senegal (Nakamura, Paliwal, and Yoshida 2018). Higher living costs can drive wage infla-tion, making cities less competitive.

Despite hints of higher productivity and wages in cities and towns, a sizable share of urban residents still engages in some form of agriculture—a fact that suggests only limited structural transformation due to urbanization. About 25 percent of the urban population in Sub-Saharan Africa—and about 30 percent in Mozambique, Sierra Leone, and Tanzania—is still employed in agriculture as the main occupation, compared with 10 percent outside Sub-Saharan Africa (Henderson and Kriticos 2017). In many countries this share has been rising rather than falling (table 1.1). However, the higher proportion of primary sector activities in urban areas seems to be driven partly by the low threshold level of what defines "urban."

NEITHER LARGE CITIES NOR SMALL TOWNS ARE LIVABLE OR PRODUCTIVE, AND MIDSIZED CITIES ARE MISSING

The Sub-Saharan urban population has doubled during the past 20 years, reach-ing almost 400 million in 2016. Definitions of "urban" vary, however: in some countries, the term can mean a town with as few as 1,000 people.[2] Using such definitions uncritically can result in exaggerated estimates of the urban popula-tion and a false assumption that large primary cities dominate the scene. In fact,

TABLE 1.1 **About one-fourth of the urban population still works in agriculture**

| | SHARE OF POPULATION WORKING IN AGRICULTURE (%) | | |
| | URBAN | | NATIONAL |
	1990	2000	LAST CENSUS
Africa			
Botswana	5.9	—	26.2
Cameroon	—	21.2	61.9
Ethiopia	14.4	—	90.2
Ghana	21.9	15.2	44.0
Liberia	—	13.7	43.9
Malawi	18.8	21.1	65.8
Mali	39.3	12.7	69.7
Mozambique	43.9	36.1	76.7
Sierra Leone	—	39.9	78.3
Tanzania	37.8	27.4	65.1
Uganda	—	16.2	76.0
Zambia	10.2	18.9	75.7
Other			
Brazil	6.6	5.9	15.2
Cambodia	33.5	14.1	72.3
India	11.0	7.4	56.6
Malaysia	5.6	4.1	16.4
Thailand	5.2	14.3	56.6
Vietnam	19.4	14.4	54.0

Source: Henderson and Kriticos 2017, using IPUMS Census Database, https://international.ipums.org /international/.

primary cities are a central feature of "urban" Sub-Saharan Africa today, but they are far from dominant.

On a closer view, "urban" Sub-Saharan Africa consists less of primary cities than of smaller cities and towns, and these smaller urban areas have been growing rapidly. Although the share of urban population residing in the largest cities remained almost steady over the past 20 years, the share residing in other urban areas (outside the largest cities) has increased (figure 1.8). Today, large cities of more than 1 million people account for 34 percent of Sub-Saharan Africa's urban population; secondary cities of 250,000 to 1 million for about 15 percent; but, most striking, smaller cities and towns with fewer than 250,000 people for about 50 percent. Among the latter, small towns with fewer than 50,000 people account for almost one-third (figure 1.9).

Large cities

Moving to a larger city brings clear improvements in living standards. Early results from a residential history module fielded in Dar es Salaam and Durban show that the first move—from outside the city—is the one that had, on average, the largest impact on improving household welfare on four dimensions: access

FIGURE 1.8

The largest city share in total urban population has remained constant

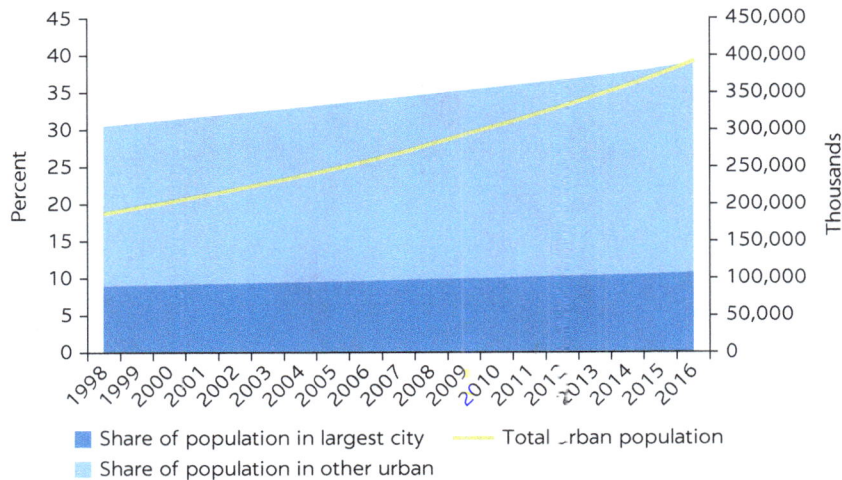

■ Share of population in largest city   ── Total urban population
■ Share of population in other urban

Source: Calculations based on World Development Indicators.
Note: Data exclude Botswana, Cabo Verde, Comoros, Equatorial Guinea, Lesotho, Mauritius, São Tomé and Príncipe, the Seychelles, and eSwatini.

FIGURE 1.9

Almost one-third of the urban population lives in towns with fewer than 50,000 people

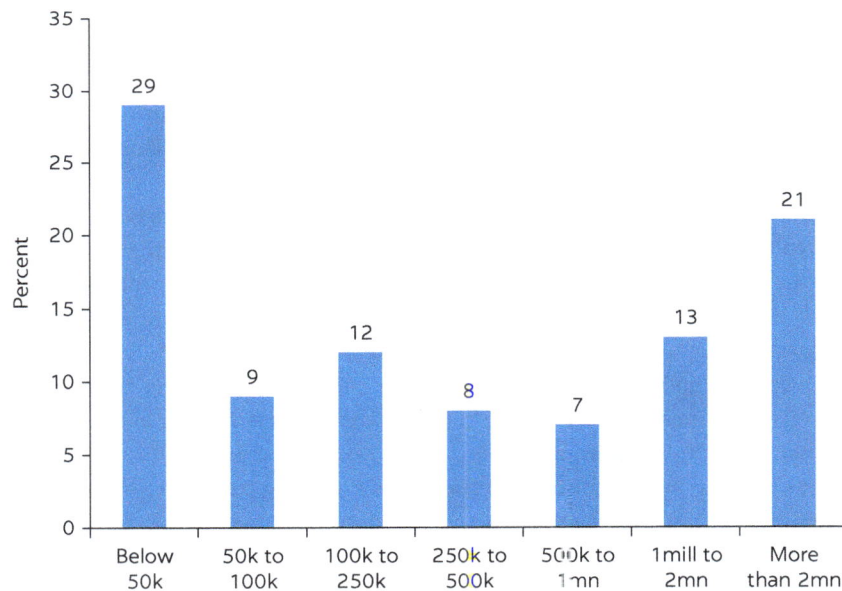

Source: Calculations based on census data from http://citypopulation.de/.
Note: Based on data for 39 countries in Sub-Saharan Africa for which censuses were available after 2004, excluding therefore Angola, the Central African Republic, Comoros, Equatorial Guinea, Eritrea, Nigeria, Somalia, and eSwatini.

to improved water, improved sanitation, durable housing, and tenure security (see figure 1.10 for Dar es Salaam).[3] Later moves within the city are less associated with such steep improvements, and, when comparing moves of residents born within Dar es Salaam, the improvements are less significant. Similar observations can be made for a similar survey fielded in Durban.

FIGURE 1.10

Biggest gains in improving living standards are made during first move to a larger city

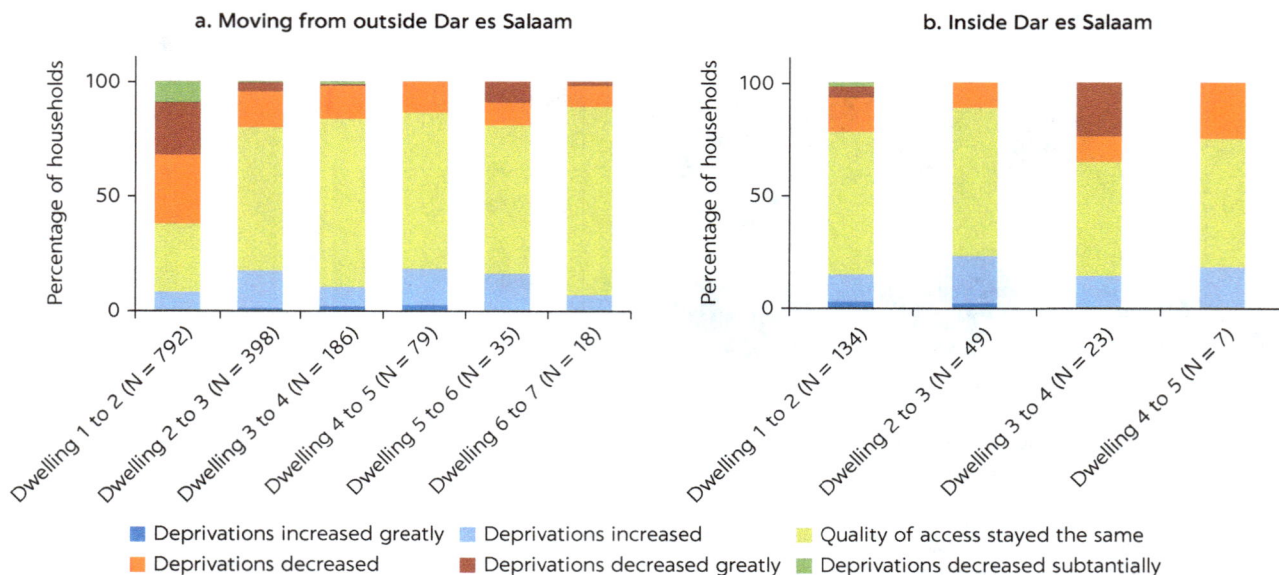

a. Moving from outside Dar es Salaam

b. Inside Dar es Salaam

- Deprivations increased greatly
- Deprivations increased
- Quality of access stayed the same
- Deprivations decreased
- Deprivations decreased greatly
- Deprivations decreased subtantially

Source: Calculated using the survey "Tanzania - Measuring Living Standards within Cities, Dar es Salaam 2014-2015 (January 10, 2019), http://microdata.worldbank.org/index.php/catalog/3399.
Note: In panel a, calculations exclude household heads who were born in Dar es Salaam and thus never moved into Dar es Salaam. By design, the first location thus reflects the average housing characteristics before moving to Dar es Salaam. Panel b includes only household heads born in Dar es Salaam, and shows the improvements in living standards households achieved during their moves within Dar es Salaam. N is the number of observations in the household survey.

Despite these improvements, even larger cities lack adequate infrastructure. For example, just about 35 percent of urban households in Sub-Saharan Africa have access to piped water, and just over 25 percent use a flush toilet (figure 1.11). Few of Sub-Saharan Africa's larger cities have a functioning sewage collection system, let alone a sewage treatment plant. Higher access rates are hence achieved only through nonnetworked options like protected dug wells or pit latrines with slab. Whether these "improved" technical solutions always fit the purpose of densely populated settlements—that is, the need to keep contamination, especially from fecal matter, out of the improved water source and for improved sanitation to clearly separate human excreta from human contact—is a serious question. Answering it requires significant monitoring of their construction and their water quality, and data for both are usually absent. Even where pipes and cables connect households to services, insufficient supply may mean that no water or electricity is provided.

For lack of alternatives, many of the urban poor reside in slums where services are worse than for the average urban resident (figure 1.12). Slum dwellers in Mombasa and Nairobi have lower access to piped water, electricity, and sanitary conditions compared with the city average. Informal settlements are densely populated, ill served by urban infrastructure, often fraught with hazards from flooding or landslides, and, by many measures, unlivable.

Living in slums is a trade-off that people in Sub-Saharan Africa make to be near their work. Without adequate and affordable transport services to connect people living farther away to their jobs, African households—more than elsewhere in the world—rely on getting to work by foot: more than 50 percent of trips are done by walking in Bamako, Conakry, Dakar, Douala, and Niamey

FIGURE 1.11
Cities lack adequate infrastructure

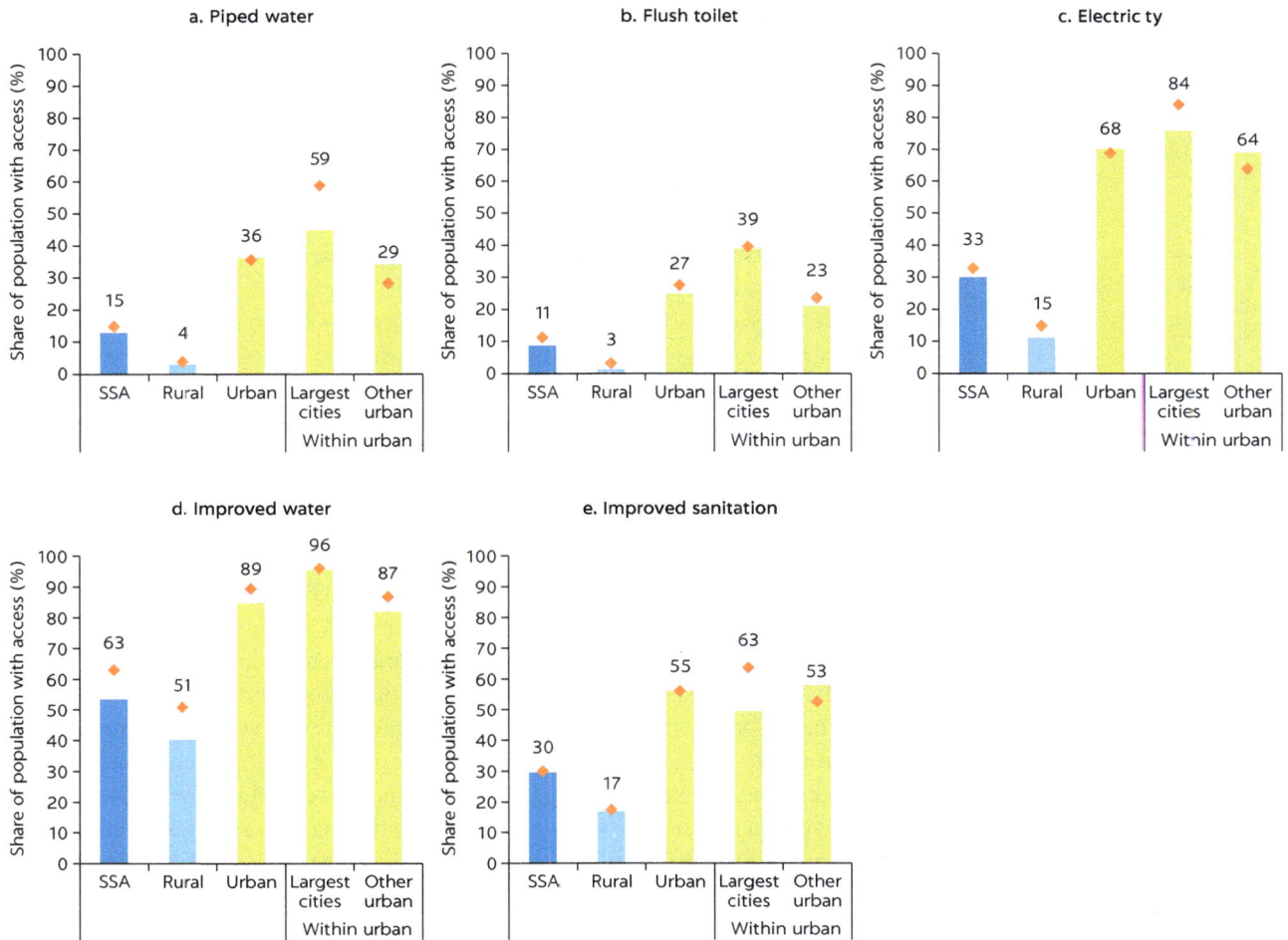

a. Piped water

b. Flush toilet

c. Electricty

d. Improved water

e. Improved sanitation

Source: Nakamura, Paliwal, and Yoshida 2018.
Note: Diamonds indicate the population share with access around 2012. Bars indicate the population share with access around 2002.
SSA = Sub-Saharan Africa.

FIGURE 1.12
Service access is unequal within cities, with slum dwellers having far less

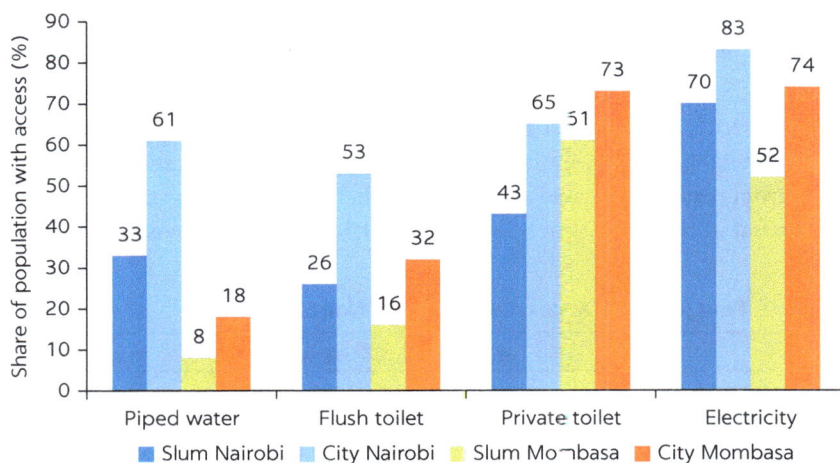

Source: Nakamura, Paliwal, and Yoshida 2018.

(Lopez-Calix, Rogy, Mukim 2018). When poorer households consider the trade-offs among housing quality, access to amenities, and other living conditions (within budget constraints), they choose to live in slums because of the proximity to central business districts and good job accessibility relative to rent values—and despite the inadequate infrastructure or access to basic services. Living closer to jobs in Nairobi increases rents dramatically, revealing that job accessibility is highly valued in the housing market there (Nakamura and Avner 2018).

The same concerns that reduce livability of cities also hamper their competitiveness. Because land use in Sub-Saharan cities is fragmented and transport infrastructure is insufficient, people are disconnected from other people and from jobs, services, and amenities. Cities fail to realize their potential gains from agglomeration and economic density, and they cannot efficiently match employers and job seekers through connections. Such inefficiency stymies agglomeration economies, keeping costs high and closing the doors of African cities to regional and global trade and investment. In Nairobi, for example, a resident can—on average—reach 4 percent of jobs in the city on foot within 45 minutes. Using a minibus increases that reach to almost 11 percent (table 1.2 and map 1.1). In contrast, a resident in Buenos Aires can reach 25 percent of jobs by public transport within 45 minutes, even though that city's urban population is four times larger than Nairobi's (Quiros-Peralta 2015).

Further concerns arise that housing, infrastructure, and other capital investments are not keeping up with the increasing size of Sub-Saharan Africa's cities. This lag has led to urban forms that do not promote competitive industries or job growth in the tradable sector. African cities develop in a fragmented and disconnected way; the underlying reason is that increased demand for land—a natural by-product of urbanization—cannot be met in most African cities because of low density, weak property rights, and poor land governance (Lall, Henderson, and Venables 2017). The result is informal urban expansions that pose challenges to urban planning and cost-effective infrastructure provision, thus deterring productive investments.

Sub-Saharan Africa's large cities are crowded, disconnected, and costly, inhibiting their ability to promote the right kind of job growth. Cities can be platforms for job growth, but how a city is spatially configured and the infrastructure it offers are key determinants as to whether a city is able to generate and promote competitive industries. The World Bank's recent research on the spatial development of African cities finds that they are not economically dense and that investments in infrastructure, industrial, and commercial structures have not kept pace with the concentration of people (Lall, Henderson, and Venables 2017). These cities have developed as collections of small and fragmented neighborhoods, limiting workers' job opportunities and preventing firms from reaping scale and agglomeration benefits. They are also expensive: 55 percent of households in Sub-Saharan Africa face higher costs relative to

TABLE 1.2 **Few jobs are accessible by foot, Nairobi**

	BY FOOT (%)	BY MINIBUS (%)	BY CAR (%)
Within 30 minutes	1.8	3.9	43.7
Within 45 minutes	4.0	10.8	71.8
Within 60 minutes	7.3	23.9	88.7

Source: Nakamura and Avner 2018.

MAP 1.1
Share of accessible jobs by minibus within 60 minutes, Nairobi

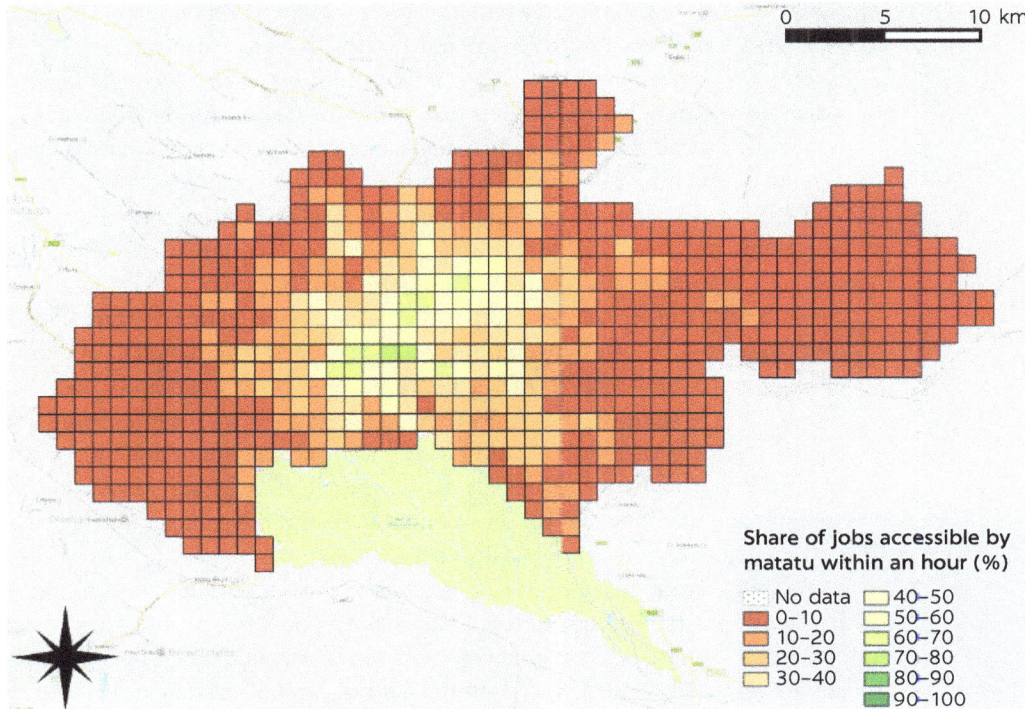

Source: Nakamura and Avner 2018.
Note: A matatu is a privately owned minibus.

other countries with comparable per capita GDP. This high cost of living raises nominal wages and transaction costs, making African industries less competitive both regionally and internationally.

Smaller towns

Most people classified as "urban" residents in Sub-Saharan Africa do not live within major urban centers. Instead, they live in the smaller towns along the city's rural fringe. These residents may have been "pushed" out of agriculture by poverty and "pulled" to smaller towns by the prospect of better access to basic services, especially education. Or they may happen to be longtime residents of formerly rural areas that later became urban. In both cases, people who were once rural and poor now probably belong to Sub-Saharan Africa's new urban poor: the number of poor is on average increasing in towns outside the largest cities.

The populations of these smaller towns outside the largest cities are growing ever larger. In Sub-Saharan countries where national urbanization levels are still recording significant increases, this growth is often due to expansion at the lower end of the hierarchy of urban areas. An estimated 30 percent of Sub-Saharan Africa's urban population lives in towns of fewer than 50,000, and this includes in most African countries' definitions of settlements with only 1,000 or 5,000 people (Henderson and Kriticos 2017).

These smaller towns face two main challenges to becoming more livable: urban service provision and formal institutions to govern land use. First, urban service delivery is efficient on a larger scale but less so on a smaller scale. The cost per person for connective infrastructure involving pipes, roads, and cables is reduced significantly with density and population numbers (Baruah, Henderson, and Peng 2017). Schools and health clinics can viably be set up and maintained only if a certain number of users can be assured. Second, efficient urban land use requires institutions that enable the formal consolidation of land into larger parcels for development, and such institutions are generally lacking in more decentralized government systems.

Tackling these constraints requires capable local institutions with the necessary remit and resources; however, mandates are too often dispersed across several layers of administrative responsibilities. In public service delivery, depending on the sector, these responsibilities may belong to a combination of central government, state-owned enterprises, and local governments. For example, in much of Sub-Saharan Africa, the responsibility for water and electricity is delegated to state-owned enterprises and responsibility for education and health to local governments—with hiring and firing still done through central governments. Small town administrations generally have a harder time attracting skills and finance to deliver services within their remit and may also lack the scale to make services economically viable.

Enabling scale and mobility in smaller towns would also require more transactional land markets for what is now poorly recorded rural land ownership. Where customary laws prevent more consolidation of land, different lease models could attract better skills and capital and may contribute to greater equity (Deininger, Savastano, and Xia 2017). Only about 10 percent of rural land ownership is currently registered: before one can contemplate more efficient land use systems and policies, land ownership needs to be demarcated and recorded in systems that can easily be administered and maintained. In Uganda, one of the more advanced countries in recording land ownership, the lack of clear property rights has removed a large proportion of land from the market: only 18 percent of private land is registered and titled. Although land registration is not necessary for tenure security, considerable international evidence suggests that it enhances tenure security by defining the nature and content of land rights, with all information on land ownership in a public record (the land registry) for inspection and its correctness assured by the state (World Bank 2012).

Residents of smaller towns are disproportionately employed in agriculture, suggesting only limited shifts into manufacturing and services due to urbanization. Although the agricultural share of employment remains significant across all urban areas, it becomes even larger for the lower hierarchy of urban systems. Other than agriculture, the other main employment basis in African towns is small trade and personal services (Henderson and Kriticos 2017). Towns' economic scope thus remains local.

As cities throughout Sub-Saharan Africa grow ever larger, developing rural-to-urban links would make sense: towns could be places that bridge rural and urban economies. Increased population growth at the lower end of the urban hierarchy—and increased concentration of the poor—has led various researchers to consider what types of economic opportunities could be exploited that offer employment to this growing population outside of farming (Collier and Dercon 2014; Norman, Merotto, and Blankespoor, forthcoming). The obvious start is to consider existing agricultural value chains and how much value added could be stimulated to generate off-farm employment in agro-processing (box 1.2) or other agriculture-related activities. Less clear is why this approach has not happened at scale, given Sub-Saharan Africa's agricultural potential.

Some of the constraints to building more robust rural-to-urban links coincide with making towns at this level of the urban hierarchy more livable. Among 20 cases of value chains, supply-side constraints for raw materials and skills are mentioned alongside location characteristics, such as weak institutions, hard

BOX 1.2

Most Sub-Saharan agro-processing is small in scale, and thus inefficient and relatively unproductive

The return to economic growth in Sub-Saharan Africa since the 1990s, burgeoning urbanization, and buoyant global commodity markets now provide unprecedented market opportunities for Sub-Saharan Africa to develop a competitive agribusiness sector. Urban food markets are set to increase fourfold to exceed US$400 billion by 2030, requiring major agribusiness investments in processing, logistics, market infrastructure, and retail networks. The growing middle class also seeks greater diversity and higher quality in its diet.

Agro-processing and horticulture—like manufacturing—benefit from agglomeration economies. Governments can support agglomerations by concentrating investments in high-quality institutions and infrastructure aimed at improving agricultural productivity and agro-processing value chains. Opportunities for the agribusiness industry suggest that targeted investment in processing, logistics, market infrastructure, and retail networks could help support the development and expansion of commercial value chains throughout the region.

Today, agro-industry in Sub-Saharan Africa mostly misses scale and thus cannot weather risks easily, nor can it unleash innovation and orientation toward global markets. Agro-processing industries equally lack scale. About 75 percent of agro-processing in Sub-Saharan Africa—except in South Africa—is by micro or small enterprises that cater to low-income households within the town or neighborhood. Entrepreneurs of that size cannot take advantage of innovation to enhance productivity and resilience,

and they cannot connect to markets beyond their towns, let alone beyond country borders.

South Africa is an illuminating exception. Although the country has more than 7,000 agro-processing firms with their own commodity value chains, the sector is dominated by a few large diversified firms. A key characteristic of agro-processing in South Africa is its strong upstream and downstream links. Upstream, the sector links to primary agriculture across a variety of farming models and products. Downstream, agro-processing outputs are intermediate products (to which further value is added) and final goods (marketed through wholesale and retail chains as well as a diverse array of restaurants, pubs, bars, and fast food franchise outlets).

Turning back to Sub-Saharan Africa as a whole, even though agriculture contributes almost one-fifth of GDP, the share of agro-processing in GDP is only about 5 percent. This pattern holds even in Tanzania, where about one-third of GDP is generated by agriculture, yet agro-processing contributes only 5.6 percent to GDP. In contrast, the share of agriculture in South Africa's GDP is only 2.4 percent, but agro-processing contributes 4.3 percent.

For the most part, Sub-Saharan Africa currently relies on commodity trading rather than adding value to its commodities, which could bring more prosperous economic development. Sub-Saharan Africa's commitment to smallholder agriculture needs alternatives to advance commercialization of production and bring more reliable inputs.

Source: ACET 2017.

infrastructure (energy, roads, and water), and soft infrastructure, such as technology, information, and finance (ACET 2017). Improving scale and mobility also requires more transactional land markets and better connectivity between rural producers and urban consumers.

Africa's missing midsized cities

Secondary cities—the middle class of cities—are largely absent from Sub-Saharan Africa's urban landscape, or if present are stagnating without an industrial role. Sub-Saharan Africa clearly deviates from world trends by having most of its urban population living in either large cities of more than 1 million or in smaller towns. In absolute terms, this implies a considerable lack of secondary city development—cities that many consider to be better facilitators of labor mobility, job creation, and the transition from rural to nonrural activities. Secondary cities are growing much more slowly than the bottom 50 percent of urban settlements by size.

Although secondary cities thrive in many parts of the developing world as they receive industry decentralized from the metropolitan giants, Sub-Saharan African countries have so little industry that secondary cities have little role. Few secondary cities have substantial local specialization in manufacturing. For cities that do have local specialization, much of that industry concentration is in very traditional activities such as textiles and clothing—minor industries in Sub-Saharan Africa's export base. These cities could become competitive in world markets through better management and infrastructure investments, including interregional transportation. Given the absence of a manufacturing base in almost all cities, however, that goal seems far off.

ENVIRONMENTAL POLICIES LAG BEHIND, MAKING LIVABILITY AN EVEN MORE DISTANT GOAL

Cities in Sub-Saharan Africa are growing without regard for the natural environment, as though it were feasible to "grow now, and clean up later." This unplanned growth causes irreversible losses to natural ecosystems, with many plant and animal species losing their natural habitats. The cost of environmental degradation will severely aggravate the living conditions of today's and tomorrow's urban population. Additionally, although much urban land remains undeveloped, investment is scant in open land and green spaces that would make cities more livable.

Generally, the spatial concentration of people and assets in urban areas creates vulnerabilities. When natural hazards—storms, earthquakes, floods, landslides, and tsunamis—occur where people and assets are concentrated, the impact is amplified. Cities in low-elevation coastal zones (LECZs) and river deltas are increasingly at risk from climate change. Although mitigation strategies can reduce risk exposure and enhance resilience, they require capable institutions to plan and enforce land use and standards, as well as capital investments into drainage systems and embankments.

Urban settlements also generate negative externalities. Uncontrolled growth can incur high costs through indiscriminate degradation and loss of natural systems. The concentration of waste and sewage generation and the burning of fossil fuels in high quantities require preventive measures either through command and control or incentive regulation or through capital-intensive investments into treatment and abatement.

Unmanaged land use allows both vulnerabilities and externalities to proliferate unchecked. Rapid and unplanned urban expansion in Sub-Saharan Africa places more pressure on natural resources both in and around cities, exacerbating natural hazards while more generally degrading the natural environment.

Existing vulnerabilities and threats from climate change

The degradation of environmental assets—such as forests, rivers, coastal habitats, and wetlands—reduces a city's resilience to climate change, undermining the well-being and future economic prospects of residents. Climate change exacerbates resource scarcity (especially water) and places vulnerable communities at risk from sea-level rise and more frequent and intense storms. Developing countries already tend to be less resilient to natural disasters because of fragile economies, poverty, lack of risk awareness, and a lack of coping capacity in urban communities. The loss of forest areas and wetlands in urban catchments can increase the risk of flooding. For example, in Dar es Salaam, Tanzania, and Douala, Cameroon, the degradation and loss of mangrove forests have increased the vulnerability of coastal areas to damages from coastal storm surges (Ellison and Zouh 2012). Cities are particularly vulnerable to many of these effects because of the greater number of people, buildings, and infrastructure in areas exposed to natural hazards.

Encroachment along rivers, canals, and hillsides and into wetlands not only reduces the resilience of cities but also reduces national output. Flooding has become a mainstay for most cities in Sub-Saharan Africa, damaging property, taking and risking lives, and disrupting the economy. To give a few examples: current annual GDP loss due to urban flooding is estimated at 4.5 percent of GDP in Mozambique (INGC 2012); since the 1980s, floods and landslides in Madagascar have caused 4,435 fatalities and US$1.8 billion in damages (Hommann, Matera, and Nakamura 2018); and, in August 2017, a massive landslide and flooding in Freetown, Sierra Leone, left more than 1,000 missing or dead. Encroachment into unplanned areas not only makes assets and people vulnerable to such disasters but also reduces the hydraulic capacity of cities. For example, building unregulated structures in informal settlements has reduced the infiltration of rainfall in Kampala. Reduced infiltration has increased runoff to six times more than would occur on natural terrain in Kampala (ActionAid 2006).

Climate change can also exacerbate conflict and increase migration pressures as herders and farmers compete for finite resources in the face of water and food shortages. Climate change threatens the livelihoods of the poor and vulnerable and undermines their ability to cope with risks from extreme weather events. Low rainfall due to climate change makes access to water increasingly difficult, significantly reducing herding and agriculture opportunities, thus stirring conflicts between herders and farmers. For example, the water scarcity from changed rainfall patterns resulting from climate change contributed to the conflict in Darfur. More agricultural losses are predicted to result from climate change, with the expectation of pushing more people from rural areas into towns and cities (Barrios, Bertinelli, and Strobl 2006; Poelhekke 2011).

Particularly at risk from climate change are the fast-growing urban areas in LECZs and river deltas. The densely populated Niger delta is directly exposed to sea-level rise, storm surges, erosion, and land subsidence. Cities along the southeastern coast of the Indian Ocean, primarily in Madagascar and Mozambique, are also affected by seasonal cyclones and tropical storms that regularly cause severe damage and losses (World Bank 2010). In 2000, more than 4 million urban residents were estimated to live in Sub-Saharan Africa's LECZs.[4] Their number is expected to reach 26 million by 2030 and 110 million by 2060 (see figure 1.13).

FIGURE 1.13

Population living in LECZs will increase to 26 million by 2030, and 110 million by 2060

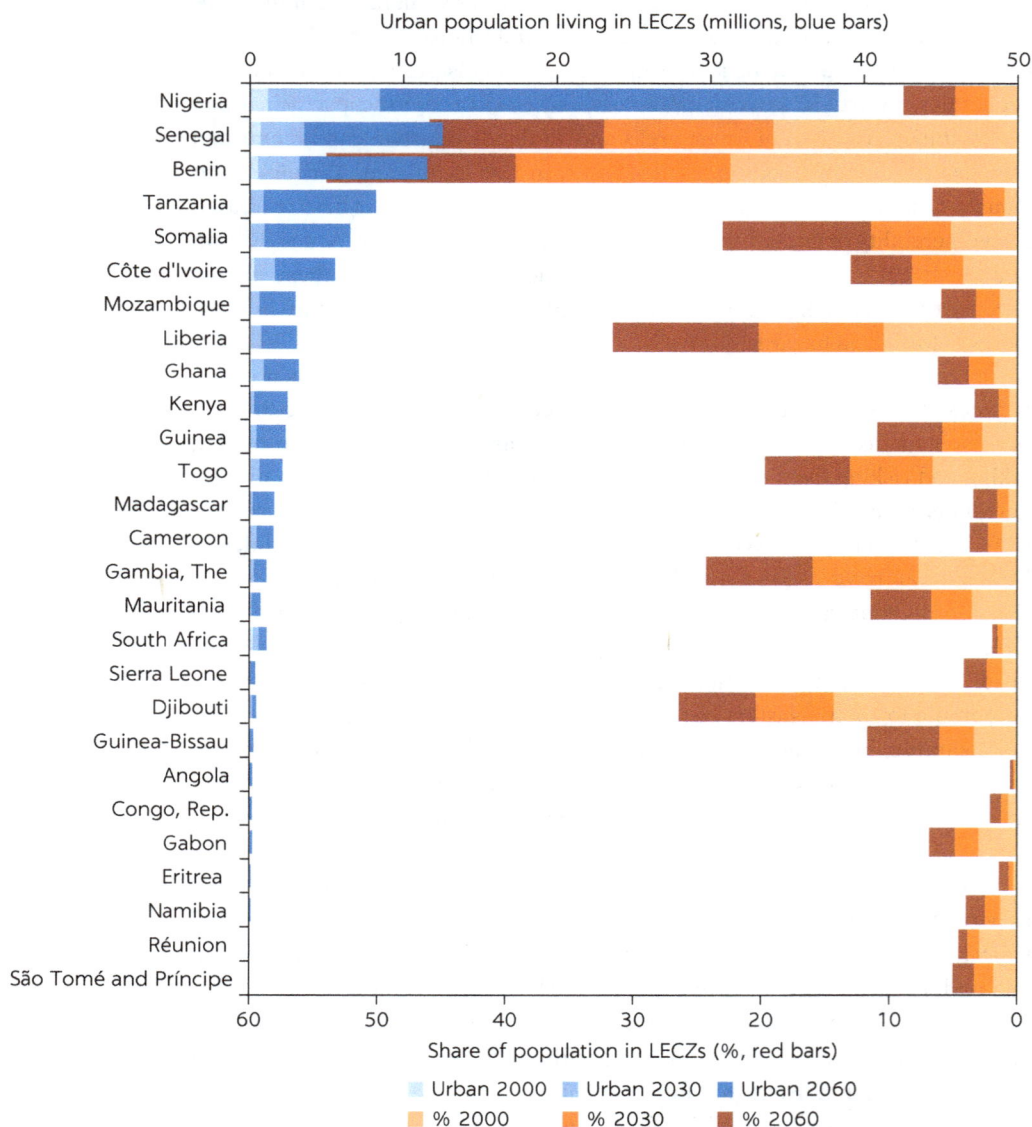

Source: Adapted from Neumann and others 2015, scenario A.
Note: LECZ = low-elevation coastal zone.

Negative externalities from concentration and encroachment

Much urban growth happens on the fringes and through unplanned and unregulated expansion, degrading ecosystems and increasing vulnerabilities. Peri-urban areas are among the fastest-growing areas—offering cheap and readily available land for settlement—but are also exposed to greater risks. Many are in precarious areas, do not adhere to planning standards or land use plans, lack adequate infrastructure, and have weak or unclear institutional structures (falling between the cracks of rural and urban local governments). For example, the metropolitan region of Dakar, Senegal, experienced the fastest population growth between 1988 and 2008 in peri-urban expansion areas, 40 percent of it on high-risk lands (map 1.2). Physical vulnerability there is compounded by weaker institutional capacity than in traditionally urban or rural areas (Wang, Montoliu-Munoz, and Gueye 2009).

Across Sub-Saharan cities, populations encroach on nearby environmentally sensitive territories, including the following examples:

- The Nakivubo wetland in Kampala has shrunk by 80 percent since 1955 through urban encroachment that harms biodiversity, endangers the city's water security, and damages its fisheries (box 1.3).
- Solid waste collection remains limited in most African cities, with collection rates below 50 percent. Where solid waste is disposed into sanitary landfills, none of the cities has guidelines on how to manage such facilities (White, Turpie, and Letley 2017).
- Lagos—like Mexico City—is sinking because of overexploitation of ground water, driven by unregulated extraction and waste in water consumption.

Negative effects on the environment are unavoidable where people concentrate; however, the extent to which this is a problem depends on regulation and investments to reduce adverse effects. Concentration of waste, sewage, and emissions from fossil fuels will inevitably lead to pollution levels beyond the normal absorptive capacity. Public awareness on the impact of inappropriate

MAP 1.2

Dakar's weak administrative capacity increases the hazard risk in peri-urban areas

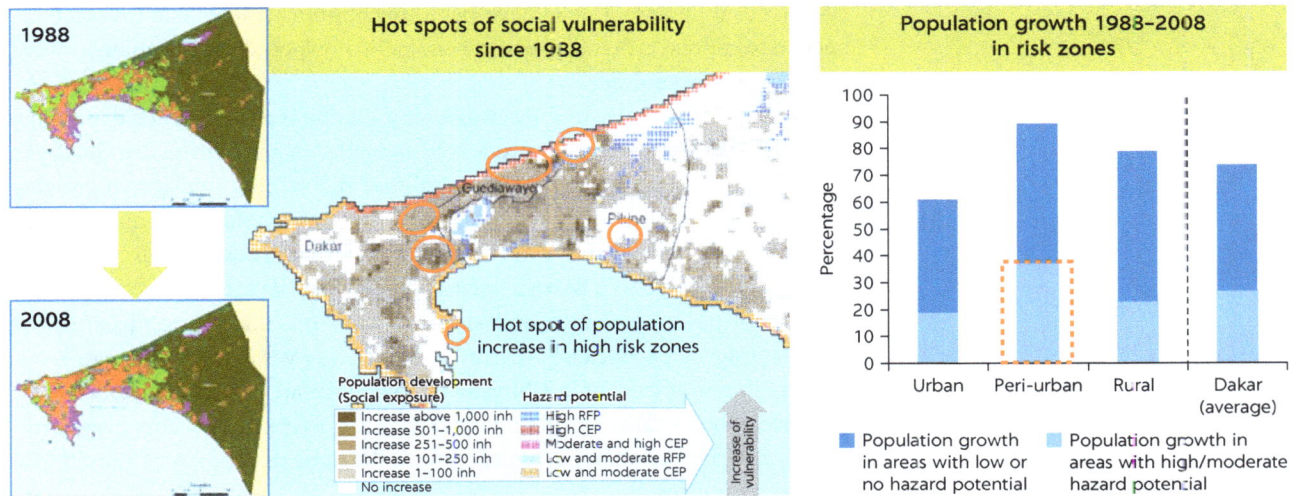

Source: Wang, Montoliu-Munoz, and Gueye 2009.
Note: Inh = inhabitants; CEP = coastal erosion potential; RFP = relative flood potential.

Lessons from Kampala's Nakivubo wetland

Where environmental assets—forests, rivers, coastal habitats, and wetlands—are degraded through urban encroachment, future economic prospects can be severely undermined. The Nakivubo wetland, one of several large wetland systems within and around the city of Kampala, is severely degraded. Polluted water from the city passes through the wetland before entering Inner Murchison Bay. In the late 1990s, the water treatment service performed by the wetland yielded a significant cost saving for the nearby Ggaba Water Treatment Works. As the city has continued to grow, however, pollution flows into the wetland have increased significantly, whereas the wetland's size and assimilative capacity have decreased. As a result, the nearby water treatment works have been upgraded twice, and new treatment works have been sited far from the city. Fisheries in Inner Murchison Bay have also all but collapsed, and the wetland itself has become the site of slum development.

These concerns, as well as the increasing shortage of public open space areas that are available for recreation in the city, have led the city to consider the

rehabilitation of the Nakivubo wetland, both to restore its functioning and to create the opportunity for a recreational area with associated possibilities for economic development. A sequential set of interventions was identified to restore the wetland to a level where economic benefits could be realized. This "treatment train" included improved sanitation infrastructure and measures, extending and upgrading the wastewater treatment works, wetland rehabilitation, conservation measures, and investment in recreational facilities. Excluding some of the required sanitation work that is already underway, the proposed fix would incur an initial cost of US$53 million, with ongoing maintenance and operating costs of US$3.6 million a year.

One of the main challenges in such interventions will be institutional. Greater Kampala extends well beyond the boundaries of the Kampala Capital City Authority, which originally encompassed the entire city. Unless the area is adjusted accordingly (as in other countries), the problems that arise in a growing city will be in areas under multiple other jurisdictions.

Source: White, Turpie, and Letley 2017.

disposal of waste has already been heightened by adverse effects on the hydraulic capacity of many cities during flood events. Likewise, hygiene messages on the paths of contamination from fecal bacteria due to absence of adequate sewage disposal and treatment have been distributed widely. The investments needed to address either disposal or treatment, however, have not come forward in the quantity required.

In comparison to waste and sewage, air pollution is a less-studied externality in the African context, and awareness of its impact is much lower. Air quality in most African countries has deteriorated (see figure 1.14), owing to a growing ownership of private motor vehicles, burning of household waste, and the continued use of charcoal and wood as primary household energy sources (White, Turpie, and Letley 2017). With few cities having formal regulations or capacities to monitor pollutants, such emissions may become a growing threat as the continent develops. Because African cities have not yet reached the high levels of air pollution prevalent in China or India, where such levels have exhibited a negative effect on labor productivity (Xu, Lozano-Gracia, and Soppelsa, forthcoming), Africa has an opportunity to avoid the same path taken by more industrialized countries.

Arguably more relevant for Africans today is indoor air pollution from cooking with solid fuels because of its severe effects on respiratory diseases. Although the

FIGURE 1.14
Nigerian cities have some of the worst air pollution

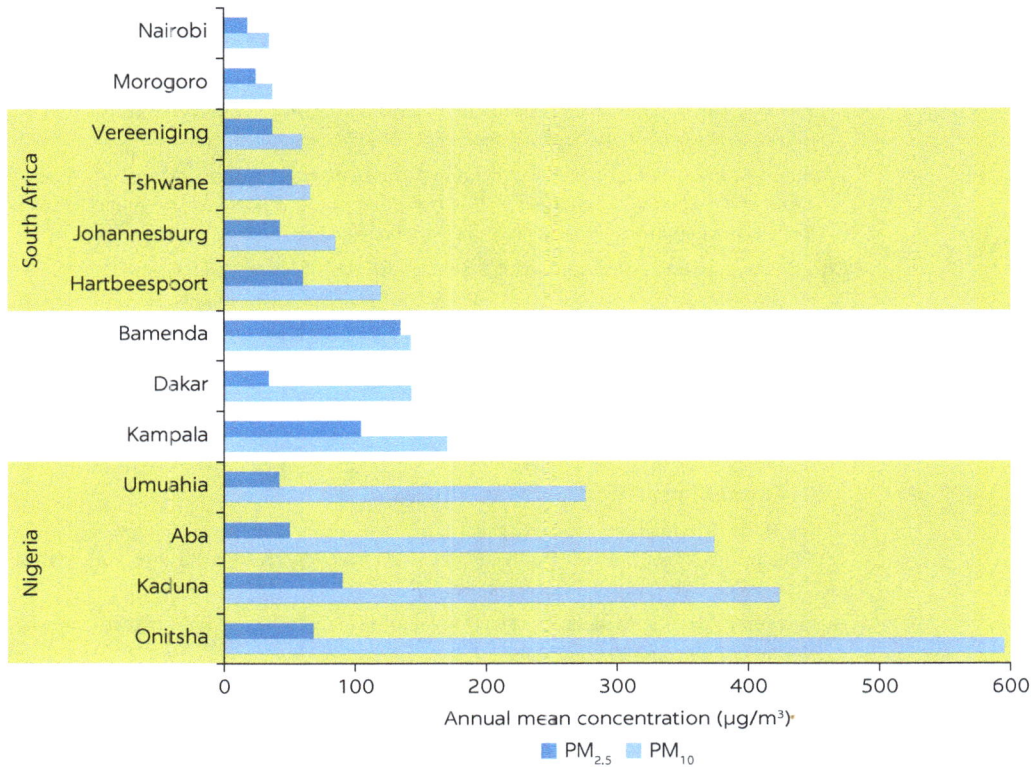

Source: White, Turpie, and Letley 2017.
Note: µg/m³ = microgram per cubic meter; PM = particulate matter less than or equal to 2.5 and 10 micrometers, respectively.

proportion of households cooking with coal and wood falls sharply with population density (Gollin, Kirchberger, and Lagakos 2017), urban households often lack the space to move their cooking to an outdoor location and therefore are less able than rural households to mitigate the negative effects of cooking with solid fuels. Respiratory diseases are thus on the rise among women and children in informal settlements of Sub-Saharan Africa (White, Turpie, and Letley 2017).

NOTES

1. Migration includes reclassification from changes in the definition of urban.
2. See annex B in Henderson and Kriticos (2017) for a list of urban definitions applied in different countries of Sub-Saharan Africa.
3. These dimensions aimed at replicating Human Habitat definitions of slums, though the residential history model had no question related to crowdedness.
4. LECZs are defined as areas less than 10 meters above mean sea level. The population living in LECZs is estimated considering sea-level rise plus 100-years-return-period storm surge.

REFERENCES

ACET (African Center for Economic Transformation). 2017. *African Transformation Report 2017: Agriculture Powering Africa's Economic Transformation*. Accra, Ghana: ACET.

ActionAid. 2006. *Climate Change, Urban Flooding, and the Rights of the Urban Poor in Africa: Key Findings from Six African Cities*. London: Action Aid.

Barrios, S., L. Bertinelli, and E. Strobl. 2006. "Climatic Change and Rural–Urban Migration: The Case of Sub-Saharan Africa." *Journal of Urban Economics* 60 (3): 357–71.

Baruah, N. G., J. V. Henderson, and C. Peng. 2017. "Colonial Legacies: Shaping African Cities." Working Paper, London School of Economics, London. https://editorialexpress.com/cgi-bin/conference/download.cgi?db_name=CSAE2018&paper_id=998.

Bocquier, P., and B. Schoumaker. Forthcoming. *The Demographic Transition in Sub-Saharan Africa and the Role of Urban Areas in This Transition*. Louvain-la-Neuve, Belgium: Centre de Recherches en Démographie, Université catholique de Louvain.

Christiaensen, L., and P. Premand. 2017. *Job Diagnostic Côte d'Ivoire: Employment, Productivity, and Inclusion for Poverty Reduction*. Jobs Series. Issue No. 2. Washington, DC: World Bank.

Collier, P., and S. Dercon. 2014. "African Agriculture in 50 Years: Smallholders in a Rapidly Changing World?" *World Development* 63: 92–101.

Deininger, K., S. Savastano, and F. Xia. 2017. "Smallholders' Land Access in Sub-Saharan Africa: A New Landscape?" *Food Policy* 67: 78–92.

Ellison, J., and I. Zouh. 2012. "Vulnerability to Climate Change of Mangroves: Assessment from Cameroon, Central Africa." *Biology* 1 (3): 617–38.

Gollin, D., M. Kirchberger, and D. Lagakos. 2017. "In Search of a Spatial Equilibrium in the Developing World." Working Paper WPS/2017-09, Centre for the Study of African Economies, University of Oxford, Oxford, U.K.

Henderson, V., and S. Kriticos. 2017. "The Development of the African System of Cities." *Annual Review of Economics* 10 (1): 287–314.

Hommann, K., M. Matera, and S. Nakamura. 2018. *Greater Antananarivo: Urban Poverty and Resilience Study*. Washington, DC: World Bank.

INGC (National Institute for Disaster Management). 2012. *Responding to Climate Change in Mozambique. Phase I, Theme 3: Preparing Cities*. Maputo, Mozambique: INGC.

Jedwab, R., L. Christiansen, and M. Gindelsy. 2017. "Demography, Urbanization and Development: Rural Push, Urban Pull and … Urban Push?" *Journal of Urban Economics* 98: 6–16.

Lall, S., J. Henderson, and A. Venables. 2017. *Africa's Cities: Opening Doors to the World*. Washington, DC: World Bank.

López-Calix, José, Michel Rogy, Megha Mukim. 2018. *The Challenges Urbanization in West Africa*. Washington, DC: World Bank. https://hubs.worldbank.org/docs/ImageBank/Pages/DocProfile.aspx?nodeid=29939753.

Lozano-Gracia, N., and C. Young. 2014. "Housing Consumption and Urbanization." Policy Research Working Paper 7112, World Bank, Washington, DC.

Nakamura S., and P. Avner. 2018. "Spatial Distribution of Job Accessibility, Housing Rents, and Poverty in Nairobi, Kenya." Paper presented to the 2018 Jobs and Development Conference, Bogota, Colombia, May 11–12.

Nakamura, S., B. Paliwal, and N. Yoshida. 2018. *Overview of the Trends of Monetary and Non-Monetary Poverty and Urbanization in Sub-Saharan Africa*. Washington, DC: World Bank.

Neumann, B., A. T. Vafeidis, J. Zimmermann, and R. J. Nicholls. 2015. "Future Coastal Population Growth and Exposure to Sea-Level Rise and Coastal Flooding—A Global Assessment." *PLOS ONE* 10 (3): e0131375. https://journals.plos.org/plosone/article?id=10.1371/journal.pone.0118571.

Norman, T., L. D. Merotto, and B. Blankespoor. Forthcoming. *It's All about the Processing: Spatial Analysis of Agro-firm Location and Jobs Potential in Zambia*. Washington, DC: World Bank.

Poelhekke, S. 2011. "Urban Growth and Uninsured Rural Risk: Booming Towns in Bust Times." *Journal of Development Economics* 96 (2): 461–75.

Quiros-Peralta, T. 2015. "Mobility for All: Getting the Right Urban Indicator." *Connections* Transport & ICT Note 25, World Bank, Washington, DC. http://pubdocs.worldbank.org/pubdocs/publicdoc/2015/11/67931446737085683/TransportICT-Newsletter-Note25a-Nov-highres.pdf.

Ravallion, M., and M. Huppi. 1991. "Measuring Changes in Poverty: A Methodological Case Study of Indonesia during an Adjustment Period." *The World Bank Economic Review* 5 (1): 57–82.

Wang, H., M. Montoliu-Munoz, and N. Gueye. 2009. *Preparing to Manage Natural Hazards and Climate Change Risks in Dakar, Senegal: A Spatial and Institutional Approach.* Washington, DC: World Bank.

White, R., J. Turpie, and G. Letley. 2017. *Greening Africa's Cities: Enhancing the Relationship between Urbanization, Environmental Assets and Ecosystem Services.* Washington, DC: World Bank.

World Bank. 2010. "Report on the Status of Disaster Risk Reduction in Sub-Saharan Africa." World Bank, Washington DC. http://www.gfdrr.org/sites/gfdrr/files/publication/AFR.pdf.

———. 2012. *Planning for Uganda's Urbanization.* Inclusive Growth Policy Note 4. Washington DC; World Bank. http://documents.worldbank.org/curated/en/353841468318588458/Planning -for-Ugandas-urbanization.

———. 2013. *Harnessing Urbanization to End Poverty and Boost Prosperity in Africa.* Washington, DC: World Bank.

Xu, C., N. Lozano-Gracia, and M. E. Soppelsa. Forthcoming. *The Effects of Pollution and Business Environment on Firm Productivity in Africa.* Washington, DC: World Bank.

2 Three Pillars on the Road toward Livable and Productive Cities: Working Land Markets, Effective Urban Planning, and Financing for Public Investments

For African cities to grow economically as they have grown in size, they must create economically efficient and productive environments to attract capital (see box 2.1). They also must create livable environments, which will in turn prevent urban costs from rising with increased population density. To enable Africa's largest cities merely to take advantage of agglomeration forces, policy makers will need to resolve basic structural problems and improve conditions for both people and businesses.

MAKING LAND MARKETS WORK—PLANNED, BUT DEMAND-DRIVEN

To become economically dense, efficient, and productive, cities require functioning land markets with formal ownership records, transfer procedures, and mechanisms for consolidating parcels in response to demand. Enabling such markets will depend on strengthening institutions. Special attention needs to be paid to land management and regulations to enable supply of serviced land, facilitate transactions, and promote higher and better use of land assets in Africa's cities. In addition, robust systems for assessing land values are key. The public sector, at both national and local levels, also plays an essential role in recording and protecting ownership claims and managing land in a fair and transparent way (figure 2.1). Most Sub-Saharan countries need to improve land management through better land use planning, a modernized land administration system, and allowing for easier and more transparent transactions (box 2.2).

A sound and effective land use planning and management system needs to be in place to correct land market distortions and to enable effective land market transactions. Proper land use planning and regulations will prevent or mitigate negative externalities, which underlie the creation of efficient and productive urban forms. To make land use regulations more effective, development controls could be complemented with financial mechanisms (such as taxes, charges, or subsidies in various modalities) to provide the incentives and disincentives to

Learning from competitive cities

The improved economic performance of competitive cities worldwide has not occurred by accident. It typically involves a strategic vision and critical action from both national and local governments.

The World Bank's global research on competitive cities shows that job creation and economic growth in cities are clearly linked to the cities' success in facilitating all three sources of private sector growth: expansion of existing firms, creation of new firms, and attraction of investors.

The review of successful cities worldwide identified four drivers of competitiveness that cities

need to invest in if they want to see economic improvement:

- institutions and regulations, infrastructure and land, skills and innovation, and enterprise support and finance

Successful cities were also found to have strong political leadership that spearheads a collective effort toward economic development, in partnership with the private sector, and sets a clear vision for the success of prominent economic subsectors.

Source: World Bank 2015a.

FIGURE 2.1

The urban land supply framework in Sub-Saharan Africa

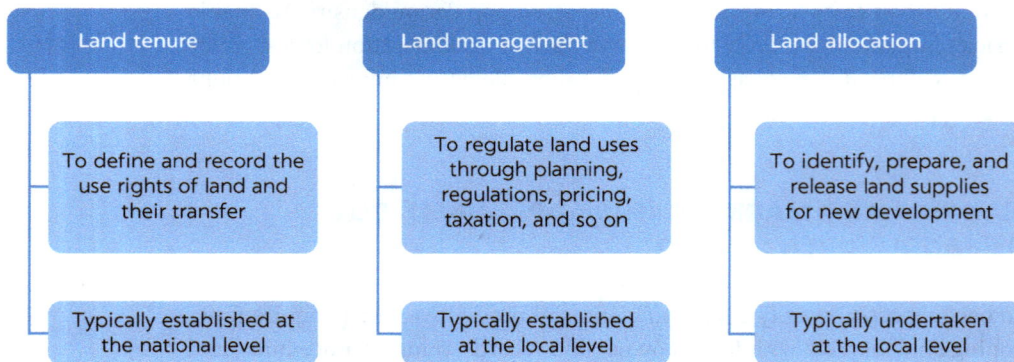

Land tenure	Land management	Land allocation
To define and record the use rights of land and their transfer	To regulate land uses through planning, regulations, pricing, taxation, and so on	To identify, prepare, and release land supplies for new development
Typically established at the national level	Typically established at the local level	Typically undertaken at the local level

Improving land management, while enhancing municipal revenue in Somaliland and Tanzania

Hargeisa, Somaliland, began in 2004 to create a land and property database, along with a methodology for classification and generating property tax invoices. Data were stored in a geographical information system (GIS) database for quick retrieval and mapping, allowing the local government to begin tax collections very quickly. The property survey, prepared in a year, was rapid and cost-effective.

The preparation cost (excluding equipment such as personal digital assistants, office computers, and software, but including the satellite image) was US$48,500 (US$0.82 per property). The new system enabled the local government to increase tax collections from US$60,000 in 2008 to US$282,725 in 2011. Since 2006, when the GIS became operational, the percentage of taxed properties has increased—from

continued

Box 2.2, *continued*

5 percent to 45 percent; the number of properties on record also increased from 15,850 to 59,000 properties over five districts. Revenue collected went into building more than 40 new roads, eight new markets, two police stations, and a land plot for a maternity and health center.

In 2014, Arusha, Tanzania, became the first of seven urban areas to switch from a manually administered own-source revenue system to a modern local government revenue-collection information system, integrated with a GIS platform. The new system allows the local government to use satellite data to identify taxpayers and includes an electronic

invoicing system that notifies and tracks payments. The city identified 102,904 buildings with this new method, compared with the 23,000 in past databases. In the 15 months since the transition to the new system, the number of eligible taxpayers tripled from 31,160 to 104,629. Within one year, the city council boosted annual revenues by 75 percent, from 2.6 billion shillings (US$1.2 million) in fiscal 2012/13 to 4.6 billion shillings in fiscal 2013/14. Supported by the new funding, the city has financed 90 percent of annual development programs including roads, drainage, school classrooms, science laboratories, health centers, and public service equipment.

Sources: Adapted from UN-Habitat 2015 and World Bank 2015b.

support implementation and enforcement. Because land is the most valuable asset of most cities, creating a land market will help boost the cities' economic growth. To that end, city administrative bodies need to work on valuing land, recording and protecting ownership rights, and managing land in a fair and transparent way.

STRONG PLANNING AND REGULATION

Urban master plans, infrastructure planning, and land use schemes must be strategic, practical, and implementable and must integrate all sectors. These plans therefore need to be translated into capital investment plans with detailed area development schemes, which also include financing options.

Effective coordination among different plans is fundamental to ensure the effectiveness of planning and the efficiency of investments. Coordination and alignment are needed both vertically across different layers of plans—including *upstream* (aligning local development initiatives with regional and national priorities, under available budgets and resources) and *downstream* (trickling down from macrolevel strategic plans to local detailed plans and leading to capital investment plans)—and horizontally across different sectors, especially between land use plans and infrastructure (particularly transport) investment plans. Such coordination requires constant engagement with economic, social, environment, and infrastructure agencies, as well as service providers, a key function of urban and regional planning.

Good urban planning practices must be visionary, inclusive, and transparent—and have built-in flexibilities. Being visionary means that these plans should aim at long-term development goals and strategies (for the next decade or two), with a forward-looking perspective identifying development trends, issues, and policies. Because no plan can be perfect, these plans need to build in sufficient flexibility in objectives and projections to better adjust to scenarios and shocks in the future, such as oil price fluctuations, natural disasters, conflicts, and influxes of displaced people. Plans could be made more flexible by allowing tweaking and adjustment according to evolving conditions; recognizing master plans and local development plans as "living documents" to be revised periodically; and enabling developers and landowners to seek changes in planning parameters (though such proposals would need to be reviewed and approved transparently and through due process).

The quality and appropriateness of planning instruments depends heavily on access to accurate information. Without such information, city leaders will be unable to plan for the future or take coordinated actions across institutions. Spearheading disruptive technologies can help largely on data collection and analysis, fostering evidence-based policy making, better governance, and efficiency. For example, in Nigeria, Sierra Leone, and Somalia, remote sensing technology has been used to estimate losses and damages in difficult-to-access places. In Kampala and Addis Ababa, satellite imagery has been used to monitor changes in land use patterns and identify vacant or underused land.

When planning urban infrastructure investments for livable cities, one step should take priority above all others: early and coordinated planning. Effective coordination of capital investments requires capable institutions. It also requires attention to the path dependency of urban forms—how cities lock themselves into spatial land use patterns that later become difficult to change—thus the significant reliance on good planning. Even in the absence of effective and functioning land markets in Africa, city leaders can leverage early investments in key infrastructure and services to shape urban forms. For example, investments in city connectivity infrastructure will determine their urban form for decades to come. Early installation of infrastructure, such as arterial road networks and catalytic bulk transport, is a practical option that enables more guided city expansion in subsequent years—especially in the absence of planning instruments. It is also cheaper in the long run, for it is less expensive and less difficult to install infrastructure before new urban dwellers have settled. In addition, urban planners and policy makers should encourage (re)development of existing infrastructure investments to shape the urban form of metropolitan growth. Clustering development around existing and planned infrastructure and services at certain spatial locations can help deliver sufficient development density to make urban services more feasible, increase land use efficiency, and enhance livability for residents.

Investment planning will differ for larger cities and for smaller towns because they often require different sets of investments. Large cities in Sub-Saharan Africa need to scale up investments in infrastructure and, as mentioned, to contend with existing infrastructure and settlements. Because of higher density, some infrastructure solutions that are acceptable to low-density environments may not be sufficient for larger cities, often requiring more capital-intensive collective solutions. Smaller towns need support for extending access to basic infrastructure services, which can be delivered either through the subnational system (where such system performs reasonably) or through direct investments.

Planning investments smartly can generate benefits that go beyond the city boundaries—an important factor to make public spending more inclusive. Analysis of Uganda's urban system reveals that a significant share of the consumption gains from investing in Kampala is outside the capital city. For example, nearly half the consumption gains from investing in Kampala's food

BOX 2.3

An integrated transport and land use planning strategy for Dar es Salaam

Dar es Salaam is East Africa's first city to implement a bus rapid transit (BRT) system, which, in just over a year of operation, has already garnered the prestigious Sustainable Transport Award from the Institute for Transportation and Development Policy. The first line of the BRT system runs along Morogoro and Kawawa Roads—one of the major development corridors of the city, which provides approximately 485,000 jobs and housing for 1.1 million people. With the development of this first BRT line, there is already an observed increase in the intensity of economic activities: developments are mushrooming and land value is rising along the corridor. This growth provides a significant opportunity for both the public and the private sectors to invest in urban development and improve the use of land along the corridor, but changes need to be carefully guided so they are appropriate contextually and culturally. In addition, a careful balance needs to be maintained to ensure that lower-income communities and the greater public also benefit from the resultant economic and social gains over time.

Under the Dar es Salaam Metropolitan Development Project, the government is working with a large group of stakeholders, supported by the World Bank and the Nordic Development Fund, to formulate a corridor development strategy. The main objective is to develop an integrated land use and implementation plan based on international best practices to guide the detailed development and appropriate densification along the first line of the Dar es Salaam BRT corridor. The project provides transit-oriented development guidelines and pedestrian-oriented development solutions for future BRT corridors. The strategy also seeks to maximize the BRT's potential impacts for urban mobility and more sustainable development patterns. Finally, it acts as a critical pilot and demonstration project to enable data-driven decision making, bring together a diverse and complex group of stakeholders toward a common agenda, and create an institutional framework for managing investment and land development for future BRT corridors—as they are constructed and commissioned.

Source: World Bank 2017b.

processing sector are outside Kampala, in rural areas or other urban centers. This finding reflects the large number of agricultural inputs used by the consumption and food processing sector, most produced by rural farmers. In general, investing in cities improves consumption and welfare throughout urban systems. Dar es Salaam is coordinating land use planning with its new bus rapid transit lines to optimize the development and revenue potential along the transit nodes (box 2.3).

INFRASTRUCTURE INVESTMENTS—SUSTAINABLY FINANCED AND MORE EFFICIENT

Even if Sub-Saharan countries can strengthen planning and regulatory institutions to better coordinate their urban infrastructure investments, how will they finance these investments? This question has no easy answer. Absolute levels of local government revenue in Sub-Saharan Africa are generally low—South Africa being the major exception—with limited own-source revenues and modest amounts from intergovernmental transfers. Central government coffers are depleted, and local infrastructure is already financed through the government transfer system. Aid is limited and often uncoordinated. The private sector is risk averse in the face of political instability and low returns. Can Africa rely on improving efficiency in its spending alone?

Average annual infrastructure spending of Sub-Saharan countries as a percentage of gross domestic product (GDP) is equal to 2 percent—lower than any other advanced economy with much higher GDP and better infrastructure to start with. According to data from 24 countries in Sub-Saharan Africa, annual public spending on infrastructure was 2 percent of GDP between 2009 and 2015. Over almost the same period (2008 to 2013), annual spending by China was 8.8 percent, by South Africa 4.7 percent, and by the United Kingdom 2.2 percent, to mention a few examples.[1] Two-thirds of spending by Sub-Saharan African countries was on roads; electricity and water supply and sanitation each accounted for one-sixth. Such public spending levels for infrastructure are far too low to address the region's deficit (World Bank 2017a).

Increasing the sources of local government revenue

Local governments in Sub-Saharan Africa—as elsewhere—finance their expenditures from three types of sources: own-source revenues, chiefly property taxes and various "business taxes"; central government transfers; and borrowings. Only a handful of large cities with rich tax bases have substantial own-source revenues, and tax mandates are often related to having regional government status. Examples include Addis Ababa, Ethiopia, with US$124 in per capita revenue for fiscal 2011/12; Nairobi County, Kenya (US$118 per capita for fiscal 2015/16); and Kampala, Uganda (US$59 per capita for fiscal 2013/14). In contrast, the average local government had much lower revenue in Uganda (average US$26 per capita, excluding Kampala); Ghana (average US$14 per capita for 2015, including rural district governments); and Côte d'Ivoire (US$6 per capita for 2013).

Property tax administration in Sub-Saharan Africa is extremely poor, with astonishingly low yields. A review of nine Sub-Saharan countries found that urban councils in Uganda received only US$6 per capita for Kampala, or an average of US$4 per capita for other municipalities, and average annual receipt in Tanzania was as low as US$0.38 per capita. The reasons include central government policy constraints, weak tax administration, and political resistance. In many Sub-Saharan countries property tax rates are set, or capped, by the central government. Many local governments also lack institutional capacity to perform the critical functions of tax administration—recording, valuation, and collection—so the process fails at every stage. And property tax, as a direct tax, is particularly vulnerable to political resistance, making local governments reluctant to improve tax administration (especially enforcement).

Given low property tax revenues, most Sub-Saharan countries permit local governments to impose further taxes on business activity—though most are not explicitly called "taxes"—and these account for a larger share of local urban revenues than property taxes. Tanzania, for example, allows local government to impose a "service levy" on registered businesses at a rate of 0.3 percent of their turnover net of value-added tax. Other countries impose annual "license fees" on various business categories. (Besides property taxes and "business taxes," a few countries such as Uganda also attempt to tax income, but these revenues are low; similarly, utility service charges may be assessed but are typically too low to cover operating costs.)

FIGURE 2.2
Intergovernmental transfers as a share of total local government revenues

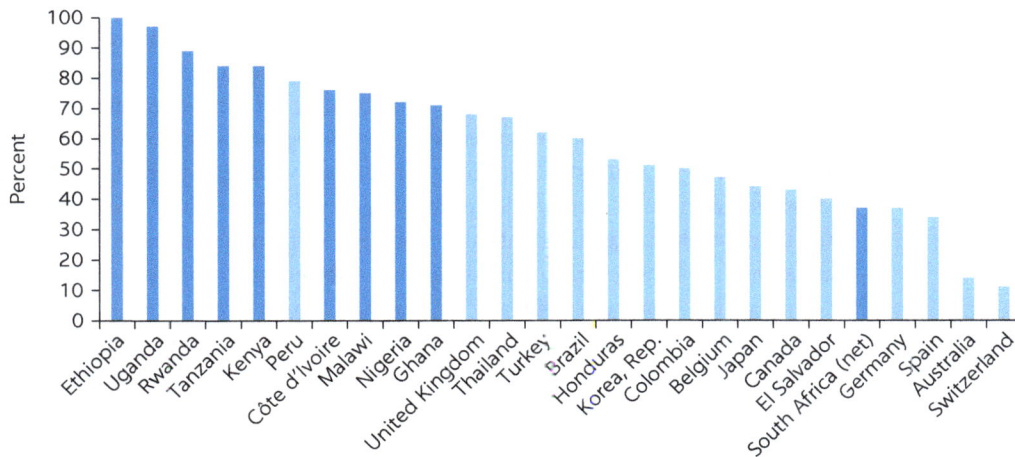

Source: Dillinger and White 2018.

With local tax revenues being low, intergovernmental transfers account for most of urban local government revenues—as much as 80–90 percent, including shared taxes (those collected by the central government but returned at least partly to the originating jurisdictions). As shown in figure 2.2, this proportion is high by international standards (a more typical share for middle- and higher-income countries would be 40–60 percent). Transfers have some beneficial effects, but they should not be a main source of local revenues. They can usefully allow central governments to set minimum service levels throughout a country and to guide local fiscal behavior through earmarking; however, they also enable local governments—especially in Sub-Saharan Africa—to derive revenues from high-yielding tax bases that are and should be reserved for central governments, thus having a redistributive effect. Even though transfers are a high proportion of total local government revenue, the level of receipt is not nearly sufficient to finance capital investments at any larger scale.

Looking farther ahead, Sub-Saharan countries will need to increase own-source revenues available to local governments—but the challenges are daunting. The predominance of the informal economy in African cities makes it difficult to tax local businesses or personal income on a significant scale. And the sorry state of property tax administration—combined with the political obstacles to imposing property taxes at significant rates—suggests that it will take time to increase yields from this source. It may also call for a review of employing more land-related taxation (as opposed to property taxation) in order to simplify the burden of valuation and as a tool to incentivize better land use in prime urban areas.

Attempts to increase reliance on local taxes can start now, though any major shift in the structure of local revenues will have to come later. Where political conditions are favorable, efforts should be made to increase the yields of property and land taxes. Local governments should also pursue opportunities to increase revenues from service charges.

Tapping central government resources and foreign aid

In the short term, the best way to finance urban infrastructure is for central governments to spend more on it—both directly by investing in infrastructure projects and indirectly by scaling up transfers. Central governments have an overwhelming comparative advantage in mobilizing resources (in part because they are the negotiators of foreign assistance, an important source of funding for most Sub-Saharan countries, with the share of the overall capital budget allocations funded through foreign aid registering 36 percent in 2015) (World Bank 2017a). Most central governments also monopolize the main tax instruments, as they should, so local governments should not appropriate these instruments.

Foreign aid in support of transfers through the government systems may support better coordination of investments at the local level and increase accountability and ownership. With major infrastructure projects being mostly undertaken directly by central government ministries or parastatals, the result often triggers poor coordination and lack of institutional coherence with local government efforts. Countries have experimented with different types of transfers for capital investment, financed by foreign aid: a move supported by the World Bank in more than a dozen countries, with mixed results (box 2.4). Such interventions often bring important opportunities to reform the procedures for distributing these transfers, reducing the role of political considerations and making their allocation more objective and transparent.

Crowding in private sector finance

Sub-Saharan Africa has seen little uptake of public–private partnerships (PPPs), particularly as far as municipal infrastructure services are concerned. Four countries (Kenya, Nigeria, South Africa, and Uganda) account for 48 percent of the PPP infrastructure projects in the region in the past 25 years. The energy sector, especially renewables, is attracting an increasing share of these projects (78 percent), followed by transport (22 percent) and water and sanitation (0.5 percent) (World Bank 2017a). This lack of PPPs largely reflects the absence of bankable projects, in which private investors could reasonably expect to make a profit. Regulatory hurdles are also an obstacle, as is political stability, which is one of the most important considerations for private investments involving sunk infrastructure. Although quasi-commercial ventures such as markets and shopping centers are potentially attractive to investors, infrastructure services generally are not. Charging for the use of municipal roads is not feasible, except in the rare cases where tolling is an option. In theory, urban water supply would be a potential candidate for PPPs. In practice, however, the management problems of existing water companies are so severe that private investors have expressed little interest, and much of the PPPs in water did not crowd in finance but were designed in the form of management contracts to institute better practice.

In principle, local governments could finance investments through municipal PPPs.[2] In Tanzania, for example, several urban local governments have agreements with private investors to provide bus terminals, municipal markets, shopping centers, and hotel and conference centers. The private partners assumed responsibility for building and operating the facility. In some instances, local governments contributed to the construction cost or provided the land. The agreements establish the share of revenues, standards for maintenance and

BOX 2.4

World Bank–supported performance-based grant projects

Since the early 2000s, the World Bank has used performance-based grants as a vehicle for financing urban local government investment projects. The projects are designed to encourage local management reforms by providing grants to local governments that achieve certain management standards. The World Bank has approved more than a dozen such operations, including several repeater projects in Ethiopia, Tanzania, and Uganda.

One of the first projects of this type was the Uganda Local Government Development Project, approved in 1999, followed by the Uganda Second Local Government Development Project in 2003. Both projects provided resources for physical investments in block grants from the central government. At the start of each project, an indicative amount was allocated to each candidate local government on the basis of population, land area, and poverty head count. To qualify for the grants, districts and urban councils were required to meet a set of minimum institutional, financial, and operational requirements. A 20 percent bonus was granted to any local government that exceeded national averages in certain thematic areas. Penalties (in the form of reduced allocations) were imposed on local governments that fell below the national averages.

Although the projects were initially successful in building administrative capacity in local governments, local government performance began to deteriorate in 2007. The 2008 National Assessment, carried out immediately after project closing, showed that only 84 local governments of the national total of 1,105 at the time earned rewards, whereas 931 were penalized because of declining quality of record keeping, meager revenue collection, weak budgeting and planning, widespread use of force accounts against procurement regulations, and "a more general lack of interest in the national assessment itself" (Dillinger and White 2018).

The first two projects in Uganda were followed by similar projects in Ethiopia and Tanzania. According to their respective implementation completion reports, both projects were largely successful. In Tanzania, the percentage of participating local government authorities meeting the minimum conditions reached 97 percent. The Ethiopia operation also substantially achieved its objectives. All 19 participating urban local governments prepared three-year rolling budgets, annual financial reports in the required format, revenue enhancement plans, and infrastructure asset inventories that were updated annually, as targeted.

In Tanzania, the system took longer than expected to set up (the project's closing date was ultimately extended by four years), and the costs of the annual assessments were high—averaging US\$1 million a year. Some key stakeholders considered that amount to be unsustainable whereas others considered the independent assessments critical to the integrity of the process. In Ethiopia, not all the positive outcomes associated with the project can be attributed to the project, in view of complementary urban sector activities. Addis Ababa performed poorly under the project, only twice attaining a "satisfactory" rating in the annual performance assessment, because the program's per capita funding for Addis Ababa was not sufficient to serve as an incentive.

operations of the facilities, and the penalties for not meeting the terms and conditions of the agreement.

To crowd in larger infrastructure investments, more innovative fund and deal structures need to be offered to mitigate risk. These structures could include guarantees and other risk-sharing designs, or blended finance instruments that can leverage private sector funding for infrastructure development.

Increasing spending efficiency

If infrastructure investment spending is to be scaled up, enhancing public investment management (PIM) systems is critical. This improvement requires a better public financial management capacity, including countries' capacity to select and appraise projects on the basis of economic return analyses, and to monitor their implementation to minimize leakages. It also entails inclusion of operation and management expenditure for existing and future infrastructure to ensure that such expenditure systems are sufficiently budgeted, in order to avoid the early decay of built infrastructure (World Bank 2017a).

Leadership in achieving better PIM is considered critical. Although the literature offers extensive guidance on how such PIM systems should be designed (see, for example, Rajaram and others 2010), implementation often fails because of the lack of leadership support of the principles outlined there. Instituting more transparency and open budget commitments helps to both solicit broader support and bring accountability to spending authorities.

Apart from enhancing PIM capacity of institutions managing large-scale infrastructure, the allocative efficiency of central government transfers must be reconsidered. Among these transfers, the most urgent need is to reform the unconditional transfers that fail to meet any efficiency criteria. Such a reform would include four steps: first, make the total amount of central government transfers more predictable—for example, by fixing them as a percentage of total central government revenues (or of GDP); second, make criteria for distributing unconditional transfers among individual jurisdictions more transparent; third, give less weight to variables in transfer formulas that are biased against cities; and last, ensure that transfers are in fact distributed according to their enabling legislation.

NOTES

1. See page at Statistica, https://www.statista.com/statistics/566787/average-yearly -expenditure-on-economic-infrastructure-as-percent-of-gdp-worldwide-by-country/.
2. In generic terms, a municipal PPP is a contract between a municipality and a private party in which the private party assumes substantial financial, technical, and operational risk in the design, financing, building, and operation of a service.

REFERENCES

Dillinger, William, and Roland White. 2018. "The Organization and Financing of Urban Infrastructure Services in Sub-Saharan Africa." Unpublished manuscript prepared for this report.

Rajaram, Anand, Tuan Minh Le, Nataliya Biletska, and Jim Brumby. 2010. "A Diagnostic Framework for Assessing Public Investment Management." Policy Research Working Paper 5397, World Bank, Washington, DC.

UN-Habitat (United Nations Human Settlements Programme). 2015. *International Guidelines on Urban and Territorial Planning*. UN-Habitat, Nairobi, Kenya.

World Bank. 2015a. *Competitive Cities for Jobs and Growth: What, Who and How?* Washington, DC: World Bank.

——. 2015b. *The Tanzanian Strategic Cities Project: Improving Local Governments' Own Source Revenues—The Arusha Experience*. Washington, DC: World Bank.

——. 2017a. *Africa's Pulse. An Analysis of Issues Shaping Africa's Economic Future*. April 2017. Volume 15. Washington, DC: World Bank.

——. 2017b. *Phase 1 BRT Corridor Development Study*. Washington, DC: World Bank.

3 Knowledge Gaps

Although this report seeks to cover much of the existing knowledge pertaining to urbanization in Sub-Saharan Africa, many questions remain unanswered. Some of these questions may find their answers through planned work by other researchers. Others will require more extensive research beyond the scope of this overview, but which might be usefully carried out in the near future.

One of the pertinent questions that emerge from this discussion is whether urbanization in Sub-Saharan Africa is too slow—in other words, are African cities growing at a slower rate than they should? The question is motivated by the fact that service access and poverty head-count rates are far superior in larger cities than in rural and other urban areas, yet the share of large cities has remained by and large constant over the past two decades.

So why don't more people move to larger cities? Understanding better the reasons why people may not choose or may not be able to move to larger cities—where they might more easily rise out of poverty and have access to more cost-effective infrastructure services—would be an important finding to help people overcome these constraints and to enhance their mobility. Although constraints may well be related to some social sorting by ethnicity or political affiliation, they may also be due to lack of protected land rights that prevent people from moving. Or is it that the pay gap is not sufficiently high, especially because most urban residents are trapped in low-earning informal jobs?

So what are the consequences of discouraging movement? If people are prevented from coming to larger cities, would enabling those who self-select to leave rural areas—typically the more able—change Africa's structural transformation path?

Planned research that is supportive of these questions entails a rural income diagnostic to be carried out by researchers in the World Bank's poverty team in conjunction with the Gates Foundation in Burkina Faso, Liberia, Mozambique, and Sierra Leone. Similarly, wage differentials could be analyzed more broadly for countries in Sub-Saharan Africa with existing data, but cost-of-living adjustments would be important to enhance existing findings.

Another important finding from this review that would benefit from further investigation is that about one-third of urban dwellers are thought to be living in towns of fewer than 50,000 inhabitants. Rather than only applying countries' administrative boundaries—although only they would enable comparable statistics on services and poverty because they also follow administrative definitions—it would be useful to understand the location of the urban population using density maps, such as those from the Global Human Settlement Layer, and to compare overlap and disagreement between these two definitions.

Last, the rural-to-urban links need to be better understood. For example, at what level in the urban hierarchy would it be best to build such links, and how would opportunities change if countries were more economically integrated and traded agricultural produce across their borders? Would that boost the income opportunities in rural areas and give more impetus to sustained poverty reduction? These questions need to be explored in close collaboration with the agricultural and jobs team to ensure well-integrated research efforts.

www.ingramcontent.com/pod-product-compliance
Lightning Source LLC
Chambersburg PA
CBHW080428270326
41929CB00018B/3201